The Plutarch Project

Volume Seven

Pompey and Themistocles

by

Anne E. White

The Plutarch Project Volume Seven: Pompey and Themistocles

Cover photograph: Anne E. White. Cover design: Bryan White

ISBN: 978-1-7772522-0-5

CONTENTS

Introduction

These notes, and the accompanying text, **are prepared for the use of individual students and small groups following a twelve-week term. The text is** that of Thomas North's 1579 translation of Plutarch's *Lives of the Noble Greeks and Romans*, with substitutions from John Dryden's 1683 translation where it seemed useful. In other volumes, I have used brackets to mark the changes from North's translation; in this one, however, they have been omitted. **Please note** that this also means that some omissions have **not** been noted. Those using audio versions or other translations may therefore want to preview those versions for suitability.

Using the Lesson Material

The study of Pompey extends over two terms. If you prefer, you could start the year with Themistocles (since it's shorter), and then read Pompey over the remaining months.

Each study contains explanatory material before the first lesson. A little at the beginning may be useful to stir interest in the study, but it is not meant to be given all in one dose! Some lessons are divided into two or three sections. These can be read all at once or used throughout the week.

I encourage you to make the lessons your own. Use the questions that are the most meaningful to you. Remember that Charlotte Mason was satisfied with "Proper names are written on the blackboard, and then the children narrate what they have listened to."

Examination Questions

The three studies include suggestions for end-of-term examinations.

Pompey

(106-48 B.C.)

> "But Pompey...was for many occasions beloved. As, for temperance of life, aptness to arms, eloquence of tongue, faithfulness of word, and courtesy in conversation: so that there was never man that requested anything with less ill will than he, nor that more willingly did pleasure any man when he was requested. For he gave without disdain, and took with great honour."

Gnaeus Pompeius Magnus (usually called **Pompey** in English) was a statesman and general in the first century B.C., during the years that Rome was shifting from a Republic to an Empire. It was a period of both economic and military upheaval. Overseas conquests had brought many captives into Italy, and small, family-run farms now competed with larger operations based on slave labour. Less opportunity for small land owners meant that many from the lower social classes joined the army instead, and expected to be paid for it. The loyalty of these soldiers was to their general, perhaps more than to Rome itself. Pompey grew up as the son of a military commander, but, as his father was somewhat unsatisfactory as a model of character, he took Alexander the Great as his lifelong hero.

Rome could also be a dangerous place in those years. In Pompey's early life, power shifted back and forth between **Gaius Marius** and his former lieutenant **Lucius Cornelius Sulla**. Their "enemies" were repeatedly punished by **proscription**: confiscation of property and a death warrant, or exile if they could escape. Early success in battle allowed Pompey to become consul (the first time of three) without meeting the usual age requirement. In his later years, he himself was the center of a similar struggle, as he became first an ally, and then a mortal enemy, of the rising Roman superstar Julius Caesar.

The Government of the Roman Republic

Commonwealth is a general term referring to a country or city/state (like Rome), and its colonies or associated territories or countries. There are also references in this story to the **Roman empire.** The Roman Empire did not formally exist until Octavian (Caesar Augustus) became Emperor in 27 B.C. However, though it was still the era of the **Roman Republic**, Rome did have an empire because of the large amount of foreign territory it was acquiring. For clarity, we will call it the small-e **empire**.

Social Classes

There were two different types of class divisions in ancient Rome. The first was family-based, between the **patricians** (the nobility) and the **plebeians** (common people).

The second type were property- or wealth-based classes such as the ***senatores***, the wealthiest citizens, who owned large amounts of land. The next level down, the **equestrian class** (in North's translation, the **knights of Rome**), was a "business class," made up of those who could afford horses and who made up the cavalry, or soldiers on horseback, in times of war. Besides the **equestrian** class, there were three classes of property owners; and then, lowest of all, the **proletarii**.

Were the *senatores* the same as the senators?

Often, but the two were not identical. Over the centuries, both the size of the Senate and the personal requirements for membership (age, wealth) changed. Some **plebeians** became senators along with the **patricians**. Those elected to **magistracies** (see below) were also included in the Senate.

What was an aedile, a quaestor, a consul?

The elected positions, or **magistracies**, in Rome were (starting at the bottom): **quaestor**, **aedile**, **praetor**, and **consul**. (The office of **tribune** was a separate position, explained below.) There were various numbers of each of these: for example, two consuls were elected each year. Ex-consuls could become **censors**; and a consul could become **dictator** if the need (usually a great emergency) arose.

Who were the tribunes?

The duty of a non-military **tribune** (sometimes called a tribune of the **plebeians**, or **plebs**; or a "tribune of the people") was to protect the liberties of the common people from any individual or group (such as the nobles) who might take advantage of them or suppress their rights. This position was not part of the junior-senior ranking of **magistrates** such as **quaestor** and **consul**; it was an office voted on by the common people **(plebeians**), who themselves were bound by oath to protect the tribunes from harm.

Other Notes

What were the bundles of rods, or rods and axes? What did it mean to "carry the axes?"

The *fasces* was a bundle of rods, usually with an axe head protruding from its side or top. It was carried before **magistrates** as a symbol of power and authority in Rome. (It may have been occasionally put to practical use as well.) Its use led to the political term **fascism.**

Is "valiantness" a word?

In this and other *Lives*, the word used to describe one who is **valiant** is **valiantness**. Today we might prefer the word **valour** (or **valor** in

American spelling). However, **valiantness** is still accepted by dictionaries, so I have left it as is.

Pompey's Wives

Antistia, Pompey's first wife, the daughter of Antistius

Aemilia Scaura, his second wife, the stepdaughter of **Sulla**

Mucia (or Mutia) Tertia, his third wife, the mother of three children: **Gnaeus Pompeius (Pompey the Younger)**, **Pompeia Magna**, and **Sextus Pompeius**. They were divorced because of her alleged unfaithfulness.

Julia, his fourth wife, daughter of Julius Caesar

Cornelia Metella, his fifth wife, daughter of **Metellus Scipio (#2)**

A confusion of names

There are several people in this *Life* named Brutus, Domitius, Lepidus, Metellus, Piso, and Scipio; not to mention Metellus Scipio. I have tried to keep them straight by numbering them as they appear.

Top Ten Vocabulary Terms in the *Life of Pompey*

If you recognize these words, you have a head start on Plutarch's vocabulary. These definitions are not repeated in the lessons.

1. **abroad:** for us this usually means "out of the country"; but it can also mean "out of one's house," or simply "out there."
2. **barbarous:** foreign, not Roman. It is not meant to be an insult (or perhaps just a slight one).
3. **divers:** separate **or** several
4. **familiar:** close friend, companion
5. **levy:** collect, gather together
6. **practice, practise:** plan, plot, scheme. British/Canadian spelling

differentiates between the noun and the verb; Americans use **practice** for both.

7. **spoil:** rob, loot (**spoils** are treasures, loot)

8. **stay:** can mean to stop or hinder someone; sometimes means to hesitate, wait, or delay either them or yourself rather than stopping altogether. (Watch out for an opposite use in **Lesson Three**.)

9. **suffer:** allow

10. To **tarry** also means to delay, but it can also mean to wait, often to wait *for* someone.

Bonus Word: victuals: food or other supplies. Pronounced "vittles."

On the Map

Place names are listed under this heading. For consistency, I have used Dryden's spelling for places instead of North's. Charlotte Mason suggested using resources such as Dent's *Atlas of Ancient & Classical Geography*, which can be found online. A newer resource I have used is the *Historical Atlas of Ancient Rome* by Nick Constable (Checkmark Books/Thalamus Publishing, 2003).

The Pompey Podcast

For those looking for an extended narration activity, and/or one that can be used in group situations, we suggest creating a short, in-class "podcast," done either a) as if it were Pompey's era, or b) with Plutarch as commentator, looking back on history. This could include interviews, storytellers, or any other appropriate content.

Lesson One

Introduction

Plutarch himself offers the best introduction to this lesson.

> "Like as of a wrestler, who hath been counted very strong, and the chiefest in all games, having ever borne the prize away where he hath wrestled, they never record among them his childish victories and wrestlings, as things of no account: even so I am afraid to speak of the wonderful deeds that Pompey did in his youth, because they are obscured in respect of the infinite great wars and battles which he had won afterwards. For I am afraid that lest I should attempt particularly to acquaint you with his first beginnings, I should too lightly pass over his chiefest acts and most notable enterprises, which do best declare his natural disposition and singular wit."

However, he does open by describing Pompey's "first beginnings."

Vocabulary

tragedy by Æschylus: a Greek play

for many occasions: for many reasons

temperance: moderateness; restraint from extremes

being come to man's estate: as an adult

in the field: on the battlefield

against Cinna: see note in **People**

captain: Dryden translates it "general"; both refer to **Strabo**

discomposure: being disturbed

betaking themselves to their arms: grabbing their weapons

mutinous: refusing to obey orders

flatling: on his face

being his heir…: according to the law, he could be prosecuted for Strabo's crime

appropriator: thief

liked of the match: approved of the marriage

the parties were secretly assured: those involved agreed to the terms

discernible: obvious, visible

People

Marius, Sulla, Cinna: In 87 B.C., **Marius** and **Cinna** were leading troops to try to re-take the city of Rome from **Sulla**. The Senate requested the help of **Strabo's** army to try to stop them. ***A note on the spelling of Sulla:*** North and Dryden spell this name "Sylla," although other sources spell it "Sulla." The reason is that Plutarch wrote in Greek, and "Sylla" was his Greek version of the Latin name.

Strabo: Pompey's father

King Alexander: Alexander the Great

Antistius: a **praetor** who became Pompey's father-in-law

Historic Occasions

157 B.C.: Birth of Marius

138 B.C.: Birth of Sulla

115 B.C.: Birth of Crassus

106 B.C.: Birth of Pompey

100 B.C.: Birth of Julius Caesar

91-89 B.C.: The Social War, which was an internal revolt based on the issue of offering Roman citizenship to allied nations. Coincidentally, the uprising broke out in Picenum, the home region of Pompey.

88-85 B.C.: First Mithridatic War

87-84 B.C.: Cinna was elected consul four years in a row

87 B.C.: Beginning of the campaign against Cinna

87 B.C.: Death of Strabo

86 B.C.: Death of Marius

86 B.C.: Pompey married Antistia

On the Map

A map of Italy and the lands and seas around it, showing the era from approximately 90 to 80 B.C., would be helpful. If you are using Constable's *Historical Atlas of Ancient Rome*, there is such a map on pages 52-53, and, for comparison, another on pages 64-65.

Reading

Part One

The Romans seem to have loved Pompey from his childhood, with the same affection that Prometheus, in the **tragedy by Æschylus**, expresses for Hercules, when he says,

> So great a hate I bare not to the father,
> But that I love the son of him much rather.

For the Romans never showed more bitter hate against any other captain than they did unto **Strabo**, Pompey's father. Contrarywise, never any other Roman but Pompey had the people's earnest goodwill so soon, nor that in prosperity and adversity continued longer constant than unto Pompey.

In Strabo, there was one great cause of their hatred, and that was his insatiable and greedy desire of money. But Pompey, his son, was **for many occasions** beloved: his **temperance** of life, aptness to arms, eloquence of tongue, faithfulness of word, and courtesy in conversation: so that there was never man that requested anything with less offense than he, nor that more willingly did pleasure any man when he was requested. For he gave without disdain; and took with great honour. Furthermore, being but a child, he had a certain grace in his look that won men's goodwill before he spoke: for his countenance was sweet, mixed with gravity; and **being come to man's estate**, there appeared in his gesture and behaviour a grave and princely majesty. His hair also stood a little upright, and the cast and soft moving of his eyes had a certain resemblance (as they said) of the statues and images of **King Alexander**. And because every man gave him that name, he did not refuse it himself: insomuch as there were some which sportingwise did openly call him "Alexander."

[omission for mature content]

Part Two

Now Pompey being a young man, and **in the field** with his father, that was in arms **against Cinna**: there was a companion of his, called Lucius Terentius, who being bribed with money, had promised Cinna to kill him (Pompey); and other confederates also had promised to set their **captain's** tent afire. This conspiracy was revealed unto Pompey as he sat at supper, he showed no **discomposure** at it, but he drank freely, and was merrier with Terentius than of custom. So, when it was bedtime, he stole out of his own tent, and went unto his father to provide for his safety. Terentius, thinking the hour come to attempt his enterprise, rose with his sword in his hand, and went to Pompey's bed where he was wont to lie, and gave many a thrust into the mattress. After he had done that, all the camp straight was in an uproar ; and the soldiers in all haste would needs have gone and yielded to their enemy, all tearing down their tents and **betaking themselves to their arms**. Strabo, for fear of this tumult, dared not come out of his tent: notwithstanding Pompey his son ran amongst the **mutinous** soldiers, and humbly besought them with the tears in his eyes, not to do their captain this villainy, and in fine threw himself **flatling** to the ground across the gate of the camp, bidding them march over him if they had such a desire to be gone. The soldiers, being ashamed of their folly, returned again to their lodging, and changing their minds, reconciled themselves with their captain, eight hundred only excepted, which departed.

Part Three

Immediately upon the death of Strabo, Pompey **being his heir, was accused for the father** of robbing the common treasure. Howbeit he confessed, and avowed, that it was Alexander, a freed slave of his father's, that had stolen the most part of it; and he proved before the judges that he (Alexander) had been the **appropriator**. But he himself was accused of having in his possession some hunting tackle, and books, that were taken at Asculum. He confessed to having them, and said that his father gave him them when the city was taken; howbeit that he had lost them since, when Cinna returned unto Rome with his soldiers; who, breaking into his house by force, spoiled him of all that he had.

His matter had many days of hearing before definitive sentence, in which time Pompey showed himself of good spirit and understanding, more than was looked for in one of his years: insomuch he won such fame and favour by it, that **Antistius**, being praetor at that time, and judge of his matter, fell into such a liking with him, that secretly he offered him his daughter in marriage. Then that matter being by friends broken to Pompey, he **liked of the match**, and **the parties were secretly assured**. However, the secret was not so closely kept as to escape the multitude, but it was **discernible** enough, from the favour shown him by Antistius in his cause. Insomuch, when the judges gave judgement, and cleared him: all the people together, as if they had been agreed, cried out with one voice, "*Talassio, Talassio*," it being the usual and common cry they used of old time at marriages in Rome.

[omission for mature content]

Narration and Discussion

What were some of Pompey's early "life lessons?"

Plutarch gives a list of five reasons that Pompey was "beloved." Which of those talents and character qualities would you most like to be known for?

How did Pompey show intelligence and courage a) when he heard that there was a plot on his life, and b) when he was accused because of his father's wrongdoing?

For older students: There is a recurring theme in this lesson about leaders, loyalty, and the respect due to those in authority. Do all leaders deserve respect, or only those who are "virtuous?"

Creative narration #1: See "The Pompey Podcast" in the introductory notes for this study. This may be done regularly, or only when it seems to suit the lesson.

Lesson Two

Introduction

Marius died in 86 B.C., and his chief ally **Lucius Cornelius Cinna** was killed two years later. Sulla's enemy **Carbo** had been co-consul with Cinna, and he now took full control over Rome. (Plutarch describes him as a senseless tyrant.) Sulla gathered a large number of troops (with the help of supporters such as Pompey), and headed back to Rome.

Vocabulary

After that: Cinna's death was in 84 B.C., so this was some time after the events of **Lesson One**

somewhat: something or other

maliced: disliked

did set upon him…: took the opportunity to attack him

slew him presently: Plutarch's version of Cinna's death, involving the disappearance of Pompey, differs from others. What is known is that Cinna was killed in a mutiny or fight by his own soldiers.

felt the goodwill: inquired to see if there was support

which came from school…: who had barely left his school days

tribunal: place of judgement, or, in this case, more of an army recruitment center

yielded unto him: joined his army

three several places: there were three battles fought

darts: javelins

Word Trivia

centurions: officers commanding a hundred men. But only eighty of those were counted as soldiers: the rest were auxiliary officers.

legion: approximately five thousand soldiers and their officers

People

Carbo: Gnaeus Papirius Carbo, co-consul with Cinna at the time of his death. He was elected consul again two years later, along with **Marius the Younger**. Carbo continued to fight against Sulla (and Pompey); but in 81 B.C. he was arrested and sentenced to death.

Marius the Younger: the son of **Gaius Marius**, who tried to carry on his father's legacy until his own defeat and death in 82 B.C.

Carinna, Caelius, and Brutus (#1): Gaius Carrinas, Gaius Coelius Caldus, and Brutus Damasippus, supporters of **Marius**

Scipio the consul (#1): Lucius Cornelius Scipio Asiaticus, consul in 83 B.C.; a supporter of **Marius**. He was exiled after Sulla's victory.

Historic Occasions

84 B.C.: death of Marius' ally **Lucius Cornelius Cinna**

84 B.C.: Sulla returned to Italy after the **First Mithridatic War**. He landed first at **Brundisium**, and there gathered additional troops (including those led by Pompey). He eventually marched on Rome, where he was declared **dictator** in 81 B.C.

83-81 B.C.: Second Mithridatic War

82 B.C.: Battle(s) of the Aesis River. The historian Appian gives a different account of the battle than Plutarch; but it is enough to know that Carbo surrendered and that Pompey got the credit.

On the Map

Picenum: home region of Pompey

Auximum: Vetus Auximum, a colony and city in Italy

Gaul: a northern territory which included parts of France, Germany, and northern Italy

River Aesis: the northern boundary of **Picenum**. (Note: Plutarch's text says the River Arsis (or Arsia), which causes confusion.)

Reading

Part One

After that, going unto Cinna's camp, they wrongfully accused him (Pompey) for **somewhat**; whereupon he, being afraid, secretly stole away. Now when they could not find him in Cinna's camp, there ran straight a rumour abroad that Cinna had put him to death. Thereupon, they that of long time had **maliced** Cinna **did set upon him for this occasion**. But he (Cinna), thinking to save himself by fleeing, was straight overtaken by a private captain that followed him with his sword drawn in his hand. Cinna seeing him, fell down on his knees before him, and took his seal from his finger wherewith he sealed his letters, which was of great price, and offered it to him. "Tush," said the captain, "I come not to seal any covenant, but to chastise a villainous and cruel tyrant." And therewithal he thrust his sword through him, and **slew him presently**.

Thus **Cinna** being slain, **Carbo**, a tyrant yet more senseless than he, took the command and exercised it; while Sulla, meantime, was approaching, much to the joy and satisfaction of most people, who in their present evils were ready to find some comfort if it were but in the exchange of a master. For the city was brought to that pass by oppression and calamities that, being utterly in despair of liberty, men were only anxious for the mildest and most tolerable bondage.

At that time Pompey was in **Picenum** in Italy, where he spent some time amusing himself, as he had estates in the country there, though the chief motive of his stay was the liking he felt for the towns of that district, which all regarded him with hereditary feelings of kindness and attachment. He saw that the noblest men of Rome forsook their houses and goods to flee from all parts unto Sulla's camp, as unto a place of safety; but he would not go to him as a fugitive and cast away to save himself, without bringing him (Sulla) some power to increase his army. So he **felt the goodwill** of the Picentines, who willingly took his part, and rejected the messengers sent from Carbo. Among them there was one Vindius, that stepping forth, said: that Pompey **which came from school the last day**, must now in haste be a captain. But they were so offended with his speech, that they fell forthwith upon this Vindius and killed him.

Part Two

After that time, Pompey being but three and twenty years old, tarrying to receive no authority from any man, took it upon him himself; and, causing a **tribunal** to be set up in the midst of the marketplace of **Auximum**, a great populous city he expelled two of their principal men, brothers of the name of Ventidius, who were acting against him in Carbo's interest; commanding them by a public edict to depart the city; he so began to levy men, and to appoint captains, sergeants of bands, **centurions**, and such other officers, according to the form of military discipline. Then he went to all the other cities of the same district and did the like. They that took part with Carbo fled, every man; and all the rest willingly **yielded unto him**; whereby in short space he had gotten three whole **legions** together, and provisions, carts, and all manner of beasts for carriage. In this sort he took his journey towards Sulla: not in haste, or desirous of escaping observation, but by small journeys, staying still where he might hurt his enemy, causing the cities everywhere as he came to revolt from Carbo.

Three commanders of the enemy encountered him at once, **Carinna**, **Cloelius**, and **Brutus (#1)**; and drew up their forces, not all in the front, not yet together on any one part, but in **three several places** they compassed him with their armies, thinking to have made him sure at the first onset. This nothing amazed Pompey, but putting his force together in one place, he first marched against Brutus, having placed his horsemen (among the which he was himself in person) before the battle of his footmen. Now the men-at-arms of the enemy, which were **Gauls**, coming to give charge upon him, he ran one of the chiefest among them through with his lance, and slew him. The other Gauls, seeing him slain, turned their backs and broke their ranks: so that at length they all fled for life. Thereupon the captains fell out among themselves, and some fled one way, some another way, the best they could. Then the towns round about, thinking that they were dispersed for fear, all came to Pompey, and yielded themselves.

Afterwards **Scipio (#1) the consul**, coming against Pompey to fight with him, when both armies were in manner ready to join: before they came to throwing of their **darts**, Scipio's soldiers saluted Pompey's men, and went on their side. So Scipio himself was driven to flee. And finally, Carbo himself having sent after him divers troops of horsemen by the **River Aesis**: Pompey made towards them, and did so fiercely assail them that he drove them into such places as was almost impossible for horsemen to come into. Whereupon they, seeing no way to escape, yielded themselves, horse and armour, all to his mercy.

Narration and Discussion

How did Pompey plan to impress Sulla?

Why were the Romans willing to accept forced rule by Sulla? Do you think they might regret this decision later on?

Lesson Three

Introduction

Pompey was gaining recognition, saluted even by Sulla; but according to Plutarch, he still did not "glory in himself." However, he was less bashful about the power he held by the sword of Rome.

Vocabulary

miscarry: fail

environed: surrounded

lighted afoot: got off his horse and walked, as a sign of respect

resaluted: paid him the same respect

faction: political party

entertainment: treatment

put away: divorce

relics: remnants

adverse party: opposition, enemy

For when they protested: The Mamertines had been exempted from direct Roman rule; but the new rulers did not honour the old treaty.

prattle: chatter, talk meaninglessly

Word Trivia

Emperor, or Sovereign Prince: North adds this translation of *Imperator*, but Dryden does not. *Imperator* comes from the word *imperare*, to command. Sulla seems to have been greeting Pompey as

"Commander" or "Captain" rather than giving him royal status.

stay: A **stay** usually means a hindrance, but it can also mean something or someone stable, to be depended on; this seems to be what is meant here. (Those familiar with the hymn "My Hope is Built" will recognize the phrase "He then is all my hope and stay.")

People

Metellus (#1): Metellus Pius, or Quintus Caecilius Metellus Pius Scipio Nasica (c. 130 BC-63 BC), Roman general. He was the adoptive father (and uncle by marriage) of **Metellus Scipio (#2)**.

Perpenna: Roman general and supporter of Marius; executed in 72 B.C.

Domitius (#1): Gnaeus Domitius Ahenobarbus, a Roman politician and supporter of Marius; Cinna's son-in-law; died in 81 B.C.

Historic Occasions

82 B.C.: Pompey married **Aemilia Scaura** (second wife)

82-81 B.C.: Pompey overcame Marian rebels in Sicily

On the Map

Sicily: the large island at the toe of Italy's "boot"

Messina: a city in the northeastern corner of Sicily

Reading

Part One

Sulla, all this while, heard no news of these overthrows; but as soon as he understood of it, fearing least Pompey should **miscarry**, being **environed** with so many captains of his enemies, he made haste to march towards him, to aid him. Pompey, understanding of his approach, commanded his captains to arm their men and to put them in battle array, that their general might see them bravely appointed when he should present them unto him: for he looked that Sulla would do him great honour; and indeed he did him more honour than Pompey looked for. For when Sulla saw him afar off, coming towards him, and his army marshalled in so good order of battle, and such goodly men that so bravely advanced themselves, being courageous for the victory they had obtained of their enemies: he **lighted afoot**. When Pompey also came to do his duty to him, and called him *Imperator* (as much as "**Emperor, or Sovereign Prince**"), Sulla **resaluted** him with the same name, beyond all men's expectation present, little thinking that he would have given so honourable a name unto so young a man as Pompey, who had not yet been senator; and considering that he himself did contend for that title and dignity with the **faction** of Marius and Scipio (#1). Furthermore, the **entertainment** that Sulla gave him every way was answerable to his first kindness offered him. For when Pompey came before him, he (Sulla) would rise and put off his cap to him, which he did not unto many other noblemen about him. All this notwithstanding, Pompey gloried nothing the more in himself.

[omission for length]

Part Two

Now when Sulla had overcome all Italy, and was proclaimed dictator, he did reward all his lieutenants and captains that had taken his part, and did advance them to honourable place and dignity in the commonwealth, frankly granting them all that they requested of him. But for Pompey: Sulla reverencing him for his valiantness, and thinking that he (Pompey) would be a great **stay** to him in all his wars: he sought by some means to ally himself to him. Metella, his wife, being of his opinion, they both persuaded Pompey to **put away** his first wife Antistia, and to marry Aemilia, the daughter of Metella and of her first husband. (But Aemilia also was another man's wife, and with child by her husband.)

[omission for content]

This marriage fell out into a miserable tragedy, by means of the death of Aemilia, who shortly after miserably died in childbirth.

Part Three

Then came news to Sulla that **Perpenna** was fortifying himself in **Sicily**, that the island was now become a refuge and receptacle for the **relics** of the **adverse party**; that Carbo also kept the sea thereabouts with a certain number of ships: that **Domitius (#1)** also was gone into Africa: and divers other noblemen that were banished, that had escaped his proscriptions, were also in those parts. Against them was Pompey sent with a great army. Howbeit he no sooner arrived in Sicily, but Perpenna left him the whole island, and went his way. Pompey favourably dealt with all the cities which had survived great trouble and misery; and set them again at liberty, the Mamertines only excepted, which dwelt in the city of **Messina**. **For when they protested** against his court and jurisdiction, alleging their privilege and exemption founded upon an ancient charter or grant of the Romans, he replied sharply, "What do ye **prattle** to us of your law, that have our swords by our sides?"

[omission for length]

Narration and Discussion

When Pompey went to re-take Sicily for Sulla, he is said to have dealt with the people there graciously and "favourably," except for those who objected! How was his response typical of Roman rule?

In **Lesson One**, Plutarch listed reasons that Pompey was "beloved" or admired: "his **temperance** of life, aptness to arms, eloquence of tongue, faithfulness of word, and courtesy in conversation." Have you seen examples of this in the story so far?

Lesson Four

Introduction

Pompey had shown his bravery in battle, and his toughness with

Sicilian holdouts; so he was now ordered to quench a rebellion in Africa, led by Cinna's son-in-law Domitius.

Vocabulary

galleys: ships powered mainly by oars

engines of battery: war machines

craggy: rocky, rough

torrent: rushing water

discern one another: tell each other apart

People

Domitius (#1): see **Lesson Three**

Memmius: Gaius Memmius, one of Pompey's commanders, and also his brother-in-law. He was killed in battle in 75 B.C. (A cousin of Gaius Memmius the poet and tribune who later opposed the triumph of Lucullus; see Plutarch's *Lucullus* and *Cato the Younger*.)

Historic Occasions

82-81 B.C.: Pompey's campaign in Africa

On the Map

Utica, Carthage: cities in northern Africa. **Utica** was the capital city of the Roman province called **Africa.**

Reading

Part One

Pompey, being busy about these matters in Sicily, received orders to go immediately into **Africa** and to make war upon **Domitius (#1)**.

Domitius had already levied more men of war than Marius had, not long before, when he came out of Africa into Italy; and when he caused a revolution in Rome, and himself from a fugitive outlaw became a tyrant. Pompey thereupon having speedily put himself in readiness to take the seas, left **Memmius**, his sister's husband, as governor of Sicily; and so he himself embarked, and hoisted sail with six score **galleys**, and eight hundred other vessels to transport their victuals, munition, money, **engines of battery**, and all other carriage whatsoever.

Part Two

After he was landed with all his fleet, part at **Utica** and part at **Carthage**, there straight came to him seven thousand soldiers from the enemy, and yielded themselves, besides seven whole legions that he brought with him. They say moreover, that at his arrival he had a pleasant chance happened unto him to be laughed at: for it is reported that certain of his soldiers stumbled on a treasure by chance and got thereby a great mass of money. The residue of the army hearing that, thought sure that the field where this treasure was found, was full of gold and silver, which the Carthaginians had hidden there long before in time of their calamity. Pompey hereupon, for many days after, could have no rule of his soldiers; neither could he choose but laugh, to see so many thousand men digging the ground, and turning up the field: until in the end they wearied themselves, and came and prayed him then to lead them where he thought good, for they had paid well for their folly.

By this time Domitius had prepared himself and drawn out his army in array against Pompey; but there was a watercourse betwixt them, **craggy**, and difficult to pass over; and this, together with a great storm of wind and rain pouring down even from break of day, seemed to leave but little possibility of their coming together; so that Domitius, not expecting any engagement that day, commanded his forces to draw off and retire to the camp. Now Pompey, who was watchful upon every occasion, making use of the opportunity, ordered a march forthwith; and having passed over the **torrent**, fell in immediately upon their quarters. The enemy was in great disorder and tumult, and in that confusion attempted a resistance; but they neither were all there, nor supported one another; besides, the wind having veered about beat the rain full in their faces. Neither indeed was the storm less troublesome to the Romans, for that they could not clearly **discern one another**, insomuch that even Pompey himself, being unknown, escaped narrowly; for when one of his soldiers demanded of him the word of battle, it happened that he was somewhat slow in his answer, which might have cost him his life.

In fine, when he had overthrown his enemies with great slaughter (for they say, that of twenty thousand of them, there were but three thousand saved), Pompey's soldiers saluted him by the name of *Imperator*. But he answered them that he would not accept the honour of that name so long as he saw his enemies' camp yet standing; and therefore, if they thought him worthy of that name, that first they should overthrow the trench and fort of the enemies, wherein they had entrenched their camp. The soldiers when they heard him say so, went presently to assault it. There Pompey fought bareheaded, to avoid the like danger he was in before. By this means they took the camp by force, and in it slew Domitius.

After that overthrow, the cities in that country came and yielded themselves, some willingly, and others taken by force. But Pompey, being desirous further to employ his power, and the good fortune of his army, went many days' journey into the mainland; and still conquered all where he came, making the power of the Romans dreadful unto all the barbarous people of that country, the which made but small account of them at that time. He said moreover, that the wild beasts of Africa also should feel the force and good success of the Romans: and thereupon he bestowed a few days in hunting of lions and elephants. For it is reported, that in forty days' space at the uttermost, he had overcome his enemies, subdued Africa, and had established the affairs of the kings and kingdoms of all that country, being then but four-and-twenty years old.

Narration and Discussion

List some of the ways Pompey showed courage and skill in leadership.

Creative narration: Tell the story of the men who "stumbled on a treasure," and its aftermath.

Lesson Five

Introduction

When Pompey was ordered to disband his army and return to Rome, his soldiers tried to force him to start his own revolution. Pompey was unswerving in his loyalty to Sulla; and as a reward he was given a particularly honourable nickname. He also believed he had earned a triumph, although he had to do some negotiating to make it happen.

Vocabulary

discharge: dismiss

mutinies: rebellions

appease: do something to restore goodwill

required the honour of triumph: requested an official victory parade

through his young years…: Senators at that time had to be at least 32 years old.

blanked: daunted, bothered

Roman knights: see introductory notes

brought Lepidus to be consul: see note below

Word Trivia

importunate: persistent and annoying. Something "opportune" is convenient and useful (like a harbour or *portus*); "importunate" is the opposite. To "importune" someone usually means to harass them.

People

Scipio (#3): Scipio Africanus, also called **Scipio the Great**, who fought against Hannibal in 202 B.C.

Lepidus (#1): Marcus Aemilius Lepidus, father of **Lepidus (#2)** (**Lesson 24**), and **Paullus** (**Lesson 19**); elected consul with the support of Pompey. Sulla warned that Lepidus would cause trouble.

Historic Occasions

81 B.C.: Sulla declared dictator in Rome

81 B.C.: Pompey's first triumph, at the age of 25

80 B.C.: Pompey married **Mucia** (third wife)

79 B.C.: Marcus Aemilius Lepidus (#1) and **Quintus Lutatius Catulus** elected consuls for 78 B.C.

79 B.C.: Pompey fought against Lepidus

78 B.C.: death of Sulla at the age of 60

On the Map

Spain: Spain, at this time, was a Roman province called *Hispania.* It was divided into two provinces, "Nearer Spain" and "Farther Spain."

Reading

Part One

So when he returned unto the city of Utica, letters were brought from Sulla, willing him to **discharge** all his army, and to remain there with one legion only, tarrying the coming of another captain that should be sent to succeed him in the government of that country. This commandment grieved him not a little, though he made no show of it at all: but his soldiers showed plainly that they were offended. For when Pompey prayed them to depart, they began to give out broad speeches against Sulla, and told directly that they were not determined (whatsoever became of them) to forsake him, and they refused that he should trust unto a tyrant. Pompey, seeing that he could not persuade them by any reason to be quiet, rose out of his chair, and retired into his tent, weeping.

But the soldiers followed him, and brought him again to his chair of state, where he spent a great part of the day, they entreating him to remain there and command them; and he, desiring them to obey Sulla, and leave their **mutinies**. But in fine, seeing them **importunate** to press him to it, he swore he would kill himself rather than they should compel him, and scarcely even thus **appeased** them.

Hereupon it was reported unto Sulla, that Pompey was rebelled against him. Sulla, when he heard that, said to his friends: "Well, then I see it is my destiny, in mine old days to fight with children." He meant so, because of Marius the Younger, who had done him much mischief, and had besides put him in great danger.

Part Two

[Plutarch jumps quickly to Pompey's arrival at the gates of Rome.]

But afterwards understanding the truth, and hearing that all generally in Rome were determined to go and meet Pompey, and to receive him with all the honour they could: because he would go beyond them all in showing goodwill, he went out of his house to meet him, and embracing him with great affection, welcomed him home, and called him *Magnus*, that is to say, "Great"; and commanded all them that were present to give him that name also. This notwithstanding, some say, that it was in Africa this name was first given him by a common cry of all his whole army, and that afterwards it was confirmed by Sulla.

Indeed it is true that Pompey himself, being sent proconsul into Spain a long time after that, was the last that signed all his letters and commissions with the name of Pompey the Great: for this name then was so commonly known and accepted, as no man did envy it.

[omission for length]

After that, Pompey **required the honour of triumph**, but Sulla denied it, alleging that none could enter in triumph into Rome but consuls or praetors. For since **Scipio (#3)**, the first who in **Spain** had overcome the Carthaginians, never desired this honour of triumph, being neither consul nor praetor: much less should he (Pompey) stand upon demand of triumph into Rome, when that **through his young years he was**

not yet a senator: and besides, it would purchase him envy of his honour and greatness. These reasons did Sulla allege against Pompey, and told him plainly that if he were bent to stand in it, he would resist him.

All this **blanked** not Pompey, who told him frankly again how men did honour the rising, not the setting of the sun: meaning thereby, how his own honour increased, and Sulla's diminished. Sulla heard him not very perfectly what he said, but perceiving by their countenances that stood by, that they wondered at it, he asked what it was he said. When it was told him, he marvelled at the boldness of so young a man, and then cried out twice together, "Let him triumph."

Many being offended therewith: Pompey (as it is reported) to anger them more, designed to have his triumphant chariot drawn with four elephants: for he had taken many of them from those kings and princes which he had subdued. Howbeit the gate of the city being too narrow, he was driven to leave the elephants, and was contented to be drawn in with horses.

[omission for length: further controversy over Pompey's triumph]

Pompey won much favour and goodwill amongst the common people: for they were glad when after his triumph they saw him in company amongst the **Roman knights**. On the other side it spited Sulla to see him come so fast forward, and to rise to so great credit: notwithstanding, being ashamed to hinder him, he was contented to keep it to himself; until that Pompey, by force and against Sulla's will, had **brought Lepidus (#1) to be consul**, by the help and good will of the people that furthered his desire.

[omission for length: the death of Sulla. Although the Lepidus incident had cooled Sulla's friendship for Pompey, to the point of leaving him entirely out of his will, it was Pompey that arranged an honourable burial for him.]

Narration and Discussion

Why was it so important to Sulla to outdo everyone else in praising Pompey? Why did he select that particular nickname?

Sulla once counted Pompey among his most loyal supporters. What changed their relationship?

Lesson Six

Introduction

After having had such a powerful ruler as Sulla, the Roman citizens seemed unsure how to move forward after his death. Wealthy families and the "mob" (those of the lower classes who could be bribed or simply excited into committing violence) fought with and against each other, and largely ignored a series of weak elected leaders.

Pompey saw an opportunity, in such troubled times, to live up to his nickname "The Great." Unfortunately, he wasn't the only one with such plans. The Marian party had not entirely disappeared, and the new consul Lepidus (#1) intended to support those who were left.

Vocabulary

exigency: urgent need

advertising: announcing

new devices: new plans, new tricks

propound: propose

meet: proper

proconsul: proconsul was the word for governor, but it could also be a pun with "for consul"

Fortune: Fortune was the Roman goddess of luck.

shut him in: besiege him

that he might have one alone...: because he wanted to beat Sertorius by himself

caparison: an ornamental covering for a horse

booty: loot

watchword: password

Word Trivia

by colour of: a phrase often meaning "using the excuse of" or "under cover of"; here it seems to mean "by means of"

People

Catulus: Quintus Lutatius Catulus, consul for 78 B.C. with **Lepidus (#1)**

Brutus (#2): Marcus Junius Brutus the Elder, put to death in 77 B.C.

"that Brutus" (#3): Marcus Junius Brutus the Younger

Sertorius: Quintus Sertorius, instigator of the Sertorian War

Metellus Pius (#1): see previous lesson

Historic Occasions

78 B.C.: Lepidus (#1) led an uprising of the Marians and attempted to take over Rome

76-71 B.C.: War in Spain against Sertorius

75 B.C.: Battle of Sucro

On the Map

Gallia Cisalpina: or Cisalpine Gaul; the closest part of Gaul to Italy

Mutina: the area around the present-day city of Modena

Sardinia: an island in the Mediterranean

Look up the Roman province of **Spain** (**Hispania**). Can you find the cities of **Lauron** and **Valentia**?

Sucro: the present-day Spanish municipality of Albalat de la Rivera

Reading

Part One

Shortly after Sulla's death, his words of prophecy unto Pompey concerning Lepidus (#1) proved true. For Lepidus openly entered straight in arms, stirring up again those of Marius' faction whom Sulla could not be revenged of; and which lay lurking a long time, spying for occasion to rise again. True it is that his colleague and fellow consul **Catulus** (whom the best and soundest part of the people followed) was thought a marvellous honest man, both just and modest: howbeit, a better governor in peace than a good man of war, insomuch as this **exigency** required Pompey's skill and experience. So Pompey stood not doubtful which way he would dispose himself, but took part straight with the nobility and the most honest men; and was presently chosen captain of their army against Lepidus.

Lepidus had already won the greatest part of Italy, and with an army under the command of **Brutus (#2)**, kept Gaul on this side of the mountains, called **Gallia Cisalpina**. And for the rest, Pompey easily overcame it: howbeit he lay a long time before **Mutina**, besieging of Brutus.

In the meantime Lepidus marched in all haste against Rome; and, being hard at the walls, demanding the second consulship, made them afraid in the city with the great numbers of men he had about him, gathered together of all sorts. Howbeit this fear was cooled straight by a letter which Pompey wrote to Rome, **advertising** how he had ended this war without any bloodshed. For Brutus, either betraying his army, or being betrayed of it, yielded himself unto Pompey, who gave him a certain number of horsemen that conducted him to a little town upon the Po River: where the next day after, Geminius, being sent by Pompey, slew him. But hereof Pompey was greatly blamed, for that he had written letters to the Senate from the beginning of the change, how Brutus had put himself into his hands: and afterwards wrote letters to the contrary, which burdened him for putting of him to death. (This Brutus was father of **"that Brutus" (#3)** which afterwards with the help of Cassius slew Julius Caesar: howbeit the son shewed not himself so like a coward, neither in wars nor in his death, as his father did; as we have declared more at large in his *Life*.)

Furthermore, Lepidus, being driven to forsake Italy, fled into **Sardinia**, where he died.

Part Two

There remained at that time **Sertorius** in Spain, who was another manner of warrior than Lepidus, and one that kept the Romans in great awe: for that all the fugitives of the recent civil wars were fled to him, as if from the last disease of the wars. He had already overthrown many inferior captains, and was now wrestling with **Metellus Pius (#1)**, who in his youth had been a noble soldier, but now being old, made wars but slowly; and who would not courageously take present occasions offered him, which Sertorius by his nimbleness and dexterity took out of his hands. For he (Sertorius) would ever hover about him (Metellus), when he thought least of him, like a captain rather of thieves than of soldiers; and (Sertorius) would lay ambushes in every corner, and round about him: whereas the good old man Metellus had learned to fight in battle array, his men being heavy armed.

Hereupon Pompey, keeping his army always together, practised at Rome that he might be sent into Spain to aid Metellus. Although Catulus had commanded him to disperse his army, Pompey still kept them together **by colour of new devices**, and was continually about Rome in arms, until that by Lucius Philippus' means he had obtained the government of that province. They say that one of the senators, marvelling to hear Philip Lucius Philippus **propound** that matter to the Senate, asked him: 'How now Philip, dost thou then think it **meet** to send Pompey as **proconsul** (to say, "for a consul") into Spain?" "No, truly" said Philip, "not *proconsul* only, but *pro consulibus*" (to say, "for both the consuls" or "as good as two consuls"): meaning that both the consuls for that year were men of no value.

Part Three

Now when Pompey was arrived in Spain, men began straight to be carried away (as the manner is commonly where new governors be) with the hope of a thing that they had not before. Thereupon Sertorius gave out proud, bitter words against Pompey, saying in mockery, he would have no other weapon but rods to whip this young boy, if he were not afraid of this old woman (meaning Metellus, the old man).

[omission for length]

In this war **Fortune** changed diversely, as it is commonly seen in wars: but nothing grieved Pompey more than Sertorius' winning of the city of **Lauron**. For he, thinking to have **shut him (Sertorius) in**, and having given out some glorious words of the matter: he wondered, when he (Pompey) saw himself straight compassed in so that he could not stir out of the camp where he lay; and was driven besides to see the city burnt before his face. But afterwards, at a set battle by the city of **Valentia**, he slew Herennius and Perpenna, both notable soldiers and Sertorius' lieutenants, and with them ten thousand men.

Part Four

This victory so encouraged Pompey, that he made haste to fight with Sertorius alone, because Metellus should have no part of the honour of the victory. So they both met by the river of Sucro, about sunset, both being in fear lest Metellus should come: Pompey, **that he might have one alone to engage with**.

The issue of the battle proved doubtful, for a wing of each side had the better; but of the generals, Sertorius had the greater honour, for that he maintained his post, having put to flight the entire division that was opposed to him; whereas Pompey was himself almost made a prisoner; for being set upon by a strong man-at-arms that fought on foot (he being on horseback), as they were closely engaged hand to hand the strokes of their swords chanced to light upon their hands, but with a different success; for Pompey's was a slight wound only, whereas he cut off the other's hand. However, it so happened that, many now falling upon Pompey together, and his own forces there being put to the rout, he made his escape beyond expectation, by quitting his horse and turning him out among the enemy. For the horse being richly adorned with golden trappings, and having a **caparison** of great value, the soldiers quarrelled among themselves for the **booty**, so that while they were fighting with one another, and dividing the spoil,

Pompey made his escape.

The next morning by break of day, both of them again brought their bands into the field, to confirm the victory, which either of them supposed they had gotten. But Metellus came to Pompey at that present time; whereupon Sertorius went his way, and dispersed his army. When Metellus came near, Pompey commanded his sergeants and officers to put down their bundle of rods and axes which they carried before him, to honour Metellus withal, who was a better man than himself. But Metellus would not suffer them, but showed himself equal with him in that, and in all things else, not respecting his seniority, nor that he had been consul, and Pompey not (saving when they camped together, Metellus gave the **watchword** to all the camp).

[omission for length]

Narration and Discussion

How did Pompey attempt to show honour to Metellus after the Battle of Sucro?

How did his understanding of human nature help him escape from a tight spot? (Look up Luke 12:15.) What previous event might have inspired this "Trojan horse" strategy? (Hint: see **Lesson Four**.)

Lesson Seven

Introduction

Through slave rebellions and military triumphs, we see Pompey's increasing maturity and power.

Vocabulary

procure: obtain or arrange something

cohort: about 500 soldiers

disperse themselves abroad: spread themselves out

sedition and stir: uprisings

even in sport: even as a joke

tribuneship...office of the tribune: See introductory notes

Knights of Rome: see introductory notes to this study

Pompey's goodwill: Pompey's backing in the election (Pompey planned to run for one consul seat, and he wanted the other one)

pulpit for orations: place to make speeches

give place (to someone): to take second place behind someone. In this case it seems to mean "be the one to give up first."

Word Trivia

the war of the bondmen and fencers...: an uprising of slaves led by Spartacus. **Bondmen** were slaves; **enfranchised** bondmen were something like serfs, those who were free-but-not-free. **Fencers** were gladiators, forced to fight for public entertainment.

People

Lucullus: Lucius Lucinius Lucullus, a Roman general who had been a confederate of Sulla; the subject of Plutarch's *Life of Lucullus.* Lucullus was known for his love of lavish banquets, so that the word *lucullan* is used to mean *luxurious* or *gourmet.* There is a story that Pompey, unable at one point to stomach common kinds of meat, was advised by a physician to eat a thrush (a small songbird). Thrushes were out of season, but it turned out that Lucullus bred them year-round for his table. Pompey mocked such luxury and said he would get by with common food.

King Mithridates: Mithridates VI of Pontus. See also **Lesson 10**.

Perpenna: see **Lesson Four**

Crassus: Marcius Licinius Crassus, the subject of Plutarch's *Life of Crassus.* Pompey and Crassus were co-consuls for the year 70 B.C.

Historic Occasions

75-63 B.C.: Third (and final) Mithridatic War. The Roman army was led by **Lucius Licinius Lucullus** (see above note), and then by Pompey during the final four years (see **Lesson Ten**).

74 B.C.: Lucullus was consul along with **Marcus Aurelius Cotta**, the uncle of **Julius Caesar**.

73-71 B.C.: Rebellion of slaves, called the Third Servile War

71 B.C.: Pompey's second triumph, at the age of 35

70 B.C.: Pompey's first consulship (with Crassus)

Reading

Part One

Pompey, having spent the most part of his goods in this war, sent to Rome for money to pay his soldiers, threatening the Senate that if they sent him no money, he would return with his army into Italy. **Lucullus** then being consul, though Pompey's enemy, **procured** they should send him money: for he (Lucullus) practised to be sent captain against **King Mithridates**; and therefore he was afraid to give Pompey any occasion to return (who desired nothing more than to leave Sertorius, to bend his force against Mithridates, whose overthrow should be more honourable to him, and also less dangerous).

In the mean space, Sertorius died, being betrayed by those whom he thought his friends, among the which **Perpenna** was the chief man. Pompey therefore marching directly towards him; and finding how ignorant Perpenna was in his affairs: he laid a bait for him of ten **cohorts**, with orders to range up and down and **disperse themselves abroad**. The bait took accordingly, and no sooner had Perpenna turned upon the prey and had them in chase, but Pompey appeared suddenly with all his army, and joining battle, gave him a total overthrow. Most of his officers were slain in the field, and he himself, being brought prisoner to Pompey, was by his order put to death.

But herein Pompey was not to be condemned of ingratitude nor oblivion (as some do burden him) of Perpenna's friendship which was shown to him in Sicily; but rather he deserved praise to have determined so wisely for the benefit of the commonwealth. For Perpenna had in his custody all Sertorius' writings (letters from the greatest noblemen of Rome, which were desirous of change of government), willing him to return into Italy. Pompey, upon sight of these letters, fearing least they would breed greater **sedition and stir** in Rome than that which was already pacified, put Perpenna to death as soon as he could; and burnt all his papers and writings, not reading any letter of them.

Pompey remained in Spain a certain time, till he had pacified all commotions and tumults.

Part Two

He then brought his army back again into Italy; and arrived there when **the war of the bondmen and fencers, led by Spartacus**, was in greatest fury. Upon his coming therefore, **Crassus** being sent captain against these **bondmen,** made haste to give them battle, which he won, and slew 12,300 of these fugitive slaves. Notwithstanding, Fortune seemed determined to give Pompey some part of this honour: five thousand of these bondmen, escaping from the battle, fell into his hands. Whereupon he, having overcome them, wrote unto the Senate that Crassus had overcome the fencers in battle, but that he himself had plucked up this war by the roots. The Romans receiving Pompey's letters, were very glad of this news for the love they bare him. But as for the winning of Spain again, and the overthrow of Sertorius, there was no man, **even in sport**, that ever gave any man else the honour, but unto Pompey only.

Part Three

For all this great honour and love they bare unto Pompey, yet they did suspect him, and were afraid of him, because he did not disperse his army, that he would follow Sulla's steps, to rule alone by plain force.

Hereupon, there were as many went to meet him for fear, as there were that went for goodwill they bare him. But after he had put this suspicion quite out of their heads, telling them that he would discharge his army after he had triumphed: then his ill-willers could blame him for nothing else but that he was more inclined to the people than to the nobility; and that he had a desire to restore the **tribuneship of the people**, which Sulla had put down, only to gratify the common people in all he could: the which indeed was true. For the common people at Rome never longed for anything more, than they did to see the office of the tribune set up again. Yea, Pompey himself thought it the happiest turn that ever came to him, to light in such a time, to do such an act. For, had any other man prevented him of that, he could never have found the like occasion possibly to have requited the people's goodwill unto him, so much as in that.

Now therefore, his second triumph and first consulship being decreed by the Senate: that made him nothing the greater, or better man. And yet was it a shew and signification of his greatness, the which Crassus (the richest man, the most eloquent and greatest person of all them that at that time dealt in matters of state, and made more estimation of himself than of Pompey and all the rest) never durst once demand, before he had craved **Pompey's goodwill**. Pompey was very glad of his request, and had sought occasion of long time to please him: and thereupon made earnest suit unto the people for him, assuring them he would as much thank them for making Crassus his colleague and fellow consul, as he would for making himself consul.

All this notwithstanding, when they were created consuls, they were in all things contrary one to another, and never agreed in any one thing while they were consuls together. Crassus had more authority with the Senate, but Pompey had more credit with the people. For he restored to them the **office of the tribune**; and passed by edict that the **knights of Rome** should have full power again to judge causes both civil and criminal.

[omission for length]

At the end of their consulship, when misliking increased further betwixt Pompey and Crassus, there was one Gaius Aurelius, of the order of knighthood, who till that time never spoke in open assembly; but he then got up into the **pulpit for orations**, and told the people openly how Jupiter had appeared to him in the night, and had commanded him to tell both the consuls, from him, that they should not leave their charge and office before they were reconciled together.

For all these words Pompey stirred not. But Crassus first took him by the hand, and spoke openly to him before the people: "My lords, I think not myself dishonoured to **give place to** Pompey, since you yourselves have thought him worthy to be called 'The Great,' before he had any hair on his face; and unto whom you granted the honour of two triumphs before he came to be senator."

When he had said his mind, they were made friends together, and so surrendered up their office.

Narration and Discussion

In **Lesson One**, Plutarch listed reasons that Pompey was "beloved" or admired: "his **temperance** of life, aptness to arms, eloquence of tongue, faithfulness of word, and courtesy in conversation." Does one or another of these stand out at this point in his life?

How much credit should Pompey have taken for ending the slave rebellion?

Creative narration: Act out or retell the scene where Crassus and Pompey received "divine orders" to put aside their differences.

Lesson Eight

Introduction

After so much excitement and attention, Pompey found life "in the robe of peace" somewhat boring. However, he was about to be offered a new challenge.

Vocabulary

gave over to plead men's causes: stopped taking on legal cases

mean persons: common people

advocate: lawyer

obscure and depress him: decrease his power, put him down

arsenals: storehouses for weapons

sundry: various

havens and beacons: harbours and signal lights

iniquity: sin, crimes

insolent parts: rude acts

houses of pleasure: vacation homes of the wealthy

their bellies full: till they were satisfied

seignory: command

edict: proclamation, decree

venture: risk

lost his labour: lost his case

Word Trivia

furlong: 1/8 of a mile; 220 yards; about 201 meters. The word comes from a "furrow long," and it was originally used to measure the distance a team of oxen could plow without resting.

People

Gabinius: Aulus Gabinius, a tribune

Caesar: Julius Caesar, Roman politician and general

Historic Occasions

102 B.C.: Romans first began fighting back against Mediterranean pirates (often called Cilician Pirates)

78-74 B.C.: Publius Servilius Vatia Isauricus led an intensive campaign against the pirates

75 B.C.: Julius Caesar kidnapped by pirates (see the *Life of Julius Caesar*)

67 B.C.: Gabinius proposed that Pompey be sent against the pirates

On the Map

Cilicia: a Roman province in what is now the southern part of Turkey

Hercules' Pillars: the entrance to the Strait of Gibraltar

Reading

Part One

Now for Crassus, he held on his former manner of life which he had begun; but Pompey, as near as he could, **gave over to plead men's causes** anymore; and began little and little to withdraw himself from frequenting the Forum, and matters of judgement; coming seldom abroad, and when he did, he had always a great train following him. It was a rare thing also to see him anymore come out of his house, or talk with any man, without being accompanied with a great number; and he rejoiced to himself, to see that he had always such a train with him: for that made him to be honoured the more, and gave him greater countenance to see himself thus courted, thinking it a dishonour to him to be familiar with **mean persons**.

And life in the robe of peace is only too apt to lower the reputation of men that have grown great by arms, who naturally find difficulty in adapting themselves to the habits of civil equality. They expect to be treated as the first in the city, even as they were in the camp; and on the other hand, men who in war were nobody think it intolerable if in the city at any rate they are not to take the lead. And so when a warrior renowned for victories and triumphs shall turn **advocate** and appear among them in the Forum, they endeavor their utmost to **obscure and depress** him; whereas, if he gives up any pretensions here and retires, they will maintain his military honour and authority beyond the reach of envy. Events themselves not long after showed the truth of this.

Part Two

By such an occasion, the power of pirates on the sea began in the country of **Cilicia**; which was not reckoned of at the first, because it was not perceived, until they grew bold and venturous in King Mithridates' wars, being hired to do him service. And afterwards, the Romans being troubled with civil wars, one fighting with another even at Rome's gates, the sea not being looked to all this while; and by degrees enticed and drew them on not only to seize upon and spoil the merchants and ships upon the seas, but also to lay waste the islands and seaport towns. So that now there embarked, with these pirates, men of wealth and noble birth and superior abilities, as if it had been a natural occupation to gain distinction in.

Now they had set up **arsenals** or storehouses in **sundry** places; they had sundry **havens and beacons** on the land, to give warning by fire all along the sea coast; and fleets were here received that were well manned with the finest mariners, and well served with expert pilots, and composed of swift-sailing and light-built vessels adapted for their special purpose. They were so gloriously set out that men hated their excess as much as they feared their force. Their ships had gilded masts at their stems; the sails woven of purple, and the oars plated with silver as if their delight were to glory in their **iniquity**. All the seacoast over, there was no sight of anything but music, singing, banqueting, and rioting. Their ships were about a thousand in number, and they had taken above four hundred towns. They had spoiled and destroyed many holy temples that had never been touched before. They had also many strange sacrifices and certain ceremonies of religion amongst themselves: among others, the Mystery of Mithres, which is the sun.

But besides all these **insolent parts** and injuries they did the Romans upon the sea, they went a-land; and where they found any **houses of pleasure** upon the seacoast, they spoiled and destroyed them; and on a time they took two Roman praetors, Sextilius and Bellinus, being in their purple robes, with their sergeants and officers attending on them, and carried them quite away. Another time also they stole away the daughter of Antonius (a man that had received honour of triumph) as she went a-walking abroad in the fields, and she was redeemed for a great sum of money.

But yet the greatest spite and mockery they used to the Romans, was this: that when they had taken any of them and that he cried he was a citizen of Rome, and named his name, then they made as though they had been amazed, and afraid of what they had done. For they clapped their hands on their thighs, and fell down on their knees before him, praying him to forgive them. The poor prisoner thought they had done it in good earnest, seeing they humbled themselves as though they seemed fearful. For some of them came unto him, and put shoes on his feet: others clapped a gown on the back of him after the Roman fashion, for fear (said they) lest he should be mistaken another time. When they had played all this pageant, and mocked him **their bellies full**: at the last they cast out one of their ship ladders, and put him on it, and bade him go his way, he should have no hurt: and if he would not go of himself, then they would cast him overboard by force. These rovers and sea pirates had all the Mediterranean Sea at their commandment: insomuch there durst not a merchant look out, nor once traffic that sea.

And this was the only cause that moved the Romans (fearing scarcity of victuals) to send Pompey to recover the **seignory** again of the sea from these pirates.

Part Three

Gabinius, Pompey's friend, was the first man that moved that Pompey should not be only admiral, or general-by-sea, but should have absolute power to command all manner of persons as he thought good, without any account to be made of his doings in his charge. The sum of this decree gave him full power and absolute authority of all the sea from **Hercules' Pillars**; and of the mainland, the space of four hundred **furlongs** from the sea. (For the Roman dominions at that time in few places went further than that: notwithstanding, within that compass were many great nations and mighty kings.) Furthermore, it gave him power to choose of the Senate fifteen lieutenants, to give unto every one of them several provinces in charge, according to his discretion: and also to take money out of the treasury to defray the charges of a fleet of two hundred sail, with full power besides to levy what men of war he thought good, and as many ships and mariners as he desired.

This law, when it had been read once over among them, the people confirmed it with very good will. Yet the noblemen and chief of the

Senate thought that this authority did not only exceed all envy, but also that it gave them apparent cause of fear, to give such absolute power unto a private person. Whereupon, they were all against it but **Caesar**, who favoured the decree: not so much to pleasure Pompey as the people, whose favour he sought.

Finally, Catulus stood up to speak against this **edict**. The people at the first heard him quietly, because he was a worthy man. Then he began, without any shew of envy, to speak many goodly things in the praise of Pompey; and, in fine, advised the people to spare him, and not to **venture** in such dangerous wars (one after another) a man of so great account, as they ought to make of him. "If ye chance to lose him," said he, "whom have you then to put in his place?"

The people then cried out: "Yourself." Then perceiving that he **lost his labour**, seeking to turn the people from their determination: he left it there, and said no more.

Roscius rose next after him to speak, but he could have no audience. When he saw that he could not be heard, he made a sign with his fingers, that they should not give Pompey alone this authority, but join another with him. The people being offended withal made such an outcry upon it, that a crow flying over the marketplace at that instant was stricken blind and fell down amongst the people. Whereby it appeareth, that fowl falling out of the air to the ground do not fall because the air is broken or pierced with any force or fury; but because the very breath of the voice (when it cometh with such a violence, as it maketh a very tempest in the air) doth strike and overcome them.

Thus for that day, the assembly broke up, and nothing was passed; and at the day appointed when this decree should pass by voices of the people, Pompey went abroad into the country. There being advertised that the decree was passed for the confirmation of his charge, he returned again that night into the city, because he would avoid the envy they would have borne him to have seen them run out of all parts of the city unto him, to have waited on him home.

Narration and Discussion

Why is it hard for heroes to return to civilian life?

What were the arguments for and against sending Pompey against the pirates? What was the deciding point?

Creative narration: Act out the role of a "pirate employment counselor," assisting someone who is looking for a change of career.

Lesson Nine

Introduction

The pirate story continues.

Vocabulary

taking infinite pains: doing something very thoroughly and carefully

check: delay

change of victuals unlooked for: their markets were suddenly full of things to buy, since their town was the base for naval operations

deprived of his consulship: Piso (#1) was accused of hindering preparations for the campaign against the pirates, which would be grounds to have him put out of office.

rovers: pirates

use: treat

unmeet: unfit

manuring the ground: growing food

Word Trivia

shoals: Dryden uses the amusing metaphor here of a **shoal**, which usually refers to a large number of fish.

People

Piso (#1): Gaius Calpurnius Piso, consul for 67 B.C.

On the Map

Brundisium: Brindisi, on the coast of the Adriatic Sea

Athens: the capital city of Greece. In 88 B.C., Athens and other Greek city-states revolted against Rome, but their rebellion was put down by Sulla. The Roman civil wars caused damage and economic hardship in Greece.

Mount Taurus: the Taurus Mountains are in southern Turkey

Coracesium: now called Alanya, in southern Turkey

Armenia: a kingdom of western Asia, ruled at that time by **Tigranes the Great**

Achaea: a region of Greece, which later (22 B.C.) became a Roman province with Corinth as its capital. (**Bible History:** In 51/52 A.D., Paul was tried in Corinth under the Roman proconsul Lucius Junius Gallio Annaeanus.)

Reading

Part One

The next morning, Pompey came abroad, and sacrificed to the gods; and, audience being given him at an open assembly, he handled the matter so well, that they gave him many things besides to enlarge his power, almost doubling the preparation set down and appointed at the first decree. For he ordained that the commonwealth should arm him five hundred ships; and they levied for him six score thousand footmen, and five thousand horsemen; and chose besides four-and-twenty senators, which had every one of them been generals of armies; and two general treasurers also. Now it happened within this time that the prices of provisions were much reduced, which gave an occasion to the joyful people of saying that the very name of Pompey had ended the war. However, Pompey, in pursuance of his charge, divided all the seas and the whole Mediterranean into thirteen parts, allotting a squadron to each,, under the command of his officers; and having thus dispersed his power into all quarters, and encompassed the pirates everywhere, they began to fall into his hands by whole **shoals**, which he seized and brought into his harbours.

Now for them that had dispersed themselves betimes, or that otherwise could escape his general chase: they fled all into Cilicia, as bees into the beehive, against whom he would needs go himself in person with three score of his best ships. Howbeit he went not before he had scoured all the coasts of Libya, Sardinia, Sicily, and of Corsica of all the thieves which were wont to keep thereabouts: and this he did within forty days' space, **taking infinite pains**, both himself and his lieutenants.

Pompey met with some interruption in Rome, through the malice and envy of **Piso (#1)**, the consul, who had given some **check** to his proceedings by withholding his stores and discharging his sailors; whereupon he sent his fleet round to **Brundisium**, himself going the nearest way by land through Tuscany to Rome; which was no sooner known by the people than they all flocked out to meet him upon the way as if they had not sent him out but a few days before. That which made the people more joyful to see him, was the sudden **change of victuals unlooked for**, that daily came to the town out of all parts. Piso was nearly **deprived of his consulship** because of this interference: for Gabinius had the decree written, and ready to present to the people. But Pompey would not suffer it.

So, having brought all to pass as he desired, he went unto the city of Brundisium, and there took sea, and hoisted sail.

Part Two

Now though his hasty voyage, and shortness of time made him pass many good cities without coming into them: notwithstanding, he would not so pass by the city of **Athens**, but landed there, and after he had sacrificed to the gods, returned to embark again. At his going out of the city, he read two writings that were made in his praise, the one within the gate which said thus:

> The humblier that thou dost thyself as man behave.

The more thou dost deserve the name of god to have.

And the other writing was without the gate, which said:

We wished for thee, we wait for thee,
We worship thee, we wait on thee.

Part Three

Now because Pompey having taken certain of these **rovers** by sea that kept together, did **use** them gently when they required pardon, and having their ships and bodies in his power, did them no hurt at all: their other companions being in good hope of his mercy, fled from his other captains and lieutenants, and went and yielded themselves, their wives and children into his hands. Pompey pardoned all them that came in of themselves, and by that means he came to have knowledge of the rest, and to follow them where they went, whom he took in the end: but knowing that they deserved no pardon, they hid themselves. Yet the richest of the pirates had conveyed their wives, children and goods, and all others of their families **unmeet** for wars, into strong castles and little towns upon **Mount Taurus**; and such as were able to carry weapons embarked, and lay before the city of **Coracesium**; where they tarried Pompey, and gave him battle, first by sea, and there were overcome; and afterwards they were besieged by land. Howbeit shortly after, they prayed they might be received to mercy; and thereupon yielded their bodies, towns, and islands. Thus was this war ended, and all the pirates in less than three months driven from the sea wheresoever they were.

[omission]

Pompey, believing that man by nature is not born a wild or savage beast, but contrarily becometh a brute beast when he falleth to vice: and again is made tame and civil in time, changing place and manner of life (as brute beasts that being wild by nature do also become gentle and tractable, with gentler usage by continuance): he determined to draw these pirates from the sea into the upland, and to make them feel the true and innocent life, by dwelling in towns, and **manuring the ground**. Some of them therefore he placed in certain small towns of the Cilicians, that were scant inhabited, and were very glad of them, giving them land to keep them with. The city of the Solians, also in Anatolia, that not long before had been destroyed by Tigranes the king of **Armenia**: being desirous to replenish that again, he placed many of them there. He bestowed divers also in the country of **Achaea**, which at that time lacked inhabitants, and had great store of very good land.

[omission for length: the official end of the war of the pirates]

Narration and Discussion

What were the results of the victory over the pirates? Did anything surprise you?

The story about Pompey's visit to Athens may seem like a sidebar to more interesting events. Why might Plutarch have included it here?

Lesson Ten

Introduction

Manius Acilius Glabrio was the new replacement for **Lucullus** (see **Lesson Seven**), who had been fighting **Mithridates VI** of **Pontus** and **Tigranes the Great** of **Armenia** in the **Third Mithridatic War**. Mithridates had won back some territory, but neither Lucullus nor Glabrio had done much to counter him (and Glabrio was, apparently, avoiding responsibility by staying in Bithynia); so Pompey was sent in to take command.

Vocabulary

tribune of the people: see introductory notes

stuck not so much: were not so unhappy

too manifest an injury: too great an insult

inveigh: to speak with hostility

knit his brows: frowned, seemed irritated

one in the neck of another: one right after another

within precinct of his charge: within his jurisdiction

the penalties enjoined them: fines or other financial punishments

finding himself hardly handled: resenting this treatment

ado: trouble, fuss

disdain: scorn

buzzard: a bird of prey, vulture

People

Glabrio: see Introduction

Historic Occasions

74 B.C.: Rome acquired **Bithynia** as a legacy from its former king (in the hope that Rome would protect it from its enemy **Pontus**)

73-63 B.C.: Third Mithridatic War

69 B.C.: Lucullus won control of Syria

69 B.C.: The kingdoms of **Pontus** and **Colchis** rebelled against Rome

67 B.C.: Pompey sent to fight against Tigranes and Mithridates

67 B.C.: Battle of Zela (the Roman army was led by Lucullus, before the arrival of Pompey)

On the Map

Bithynia: kingdom and Roman province, located in present-day Turkey

Galatia: a region bordering on **Bithynia** and **Pontus**

Reading

Part One

When news came to Rome that the pirates' war was brought to good end, and that Pompey, having no other service in hand, went visiting the cities up and down: one Manilius, a **tribune of the people**, put forth another decree unto them of this effect:

> That Pompey, taking all the army Lucullus had, and the provinces under his government; with all **Bithynia** (which was under the command of **Glabrio)**; should go make war upon the two kings, **Tigranes** and **Mithridates**, keeping in his hands notwithstanding all his jurisdiction and army by sea, in as royal manner as he had it before.

In fine, this was even to make one man monarch and absolute prince of all the Roman empire. For by this second decree, Pompey had all these countries not named in his former commission (Phrygia, Lycaonia, Galatia, Cappadocia, Cilicia, high Colchida, and Armenia) added to amplify his authority; along with all the armies and forces with which he already had; to overcome those two mighty kings. Then the Senate **stuck not so much** at the injury that was offered unto Lucullus, depriving him of the honour of his doings, to give it to another, that should rather succeed him in honour of triumph than in danger of wars, knowing that they did him **too manifest an injury**, and shewed themselves too unthankful: but that which most grieved them was to see Pompey's power established in a plain tyranny.

Hereupon therefore, the senators persuaded and encouraged each other stoutly to withstand this edict, and not to suffer their liberty to be lost in this sort. Notwithstanding, when the day came that the decree should pass, they were so afraid to anger the people, that their hearts failed them, and none durst speak against it but Catulus only: he earnestly **inveighed** against the passing of it a long time together, and greatly blamed the people. At the length, perceiving he had won never a man to take his part, he oftentimes cried out to the Senate, that they should look to seek out some mountain or high rock to retire safely unto, to defend their liberty, as their ancestors had done in old time before them. All this prevailed not, for the decree passed by the voices of all the tribes, as it is reported.

And thus was Pompey in his absence made lord almost of all that which Sulla, by force of arms and great effusion of blood (having made himself lord of Rome), had before in his power.

Part Two

When Pompey had received letters from Rome, advertising him what the people had passed in his behalf: some say that at the receipt of them (in the presence of his familiar friends that were about him, and rejoiced with him for congratulation) he **knit his brows**, and clapped on his thigh, as though it grieved him marvellously to have such great offices and charge laid upon him, **one in the neck of another**, and burst forth in these words:

> "O gods, shall I never see an end of such a world of troubles as I have? Had it not been better for me to have been a mean man born and unknown, than thus continually to be in war with armour on my back? What, shall I never see the time, that breaking the necks of spite and envy against me, I may yet once in my life live quietly at home in my country, with my wife and children?"

But all this was looked upon as mere trifling, neither indeed could the best of his friends call it anything else, well knowing that his enmity with Lucullus, setting a flame just now to his natural passion for glory and empire, made him feel more than usually gratified. For he presently sent out proclamations into every quarter, commanding all sorts of soldiers to come to him immediately, and made also all the princes and kings **within precinct of his charge** to come unto him; and going through the countries, altered and changed all that Lucullus had established before.

Furthermore, he did release **the penalties enjoined them**, and took from them also the gifts that Lucullus bestowed of them. In fine, this was all his purpose and desire: to make them that honoured Lucullus know that he had no further power and authority to do anything: Lucullus **finding himself hardly handled** by Pompey, the friends of either side thought good they should meet and talk together: which came so to pass, for they met in the country of **Galatia**.

And because they both were great captains of the Roman armies, and had done many famous acts, they had their sergeants and officers that carried the bundles of rods before them, wreathed about with laurel boughs. When they met, Lucullus came out of a close and woody country, all covered with green trees, and Pompey on the other side had passed through a great sandy plain, where no tree was growing. Thereupon Lucullus' sergeants seeing the laurel boughs dry and withered away, which Pompey's sergeants carried, they gave them of their green and fresh boughs to beautify the rods and axes. This was a plain token that Pompey came to take Lucullus' honour from him. In truth Lucullus had been consul before Pompey, and so was he also an older man than he; yet the dignity of Pompey was greater, because he had triumphed twice.

At their first meeting, their entertainment and discourse was with great ceremony and courtesy as might be, one highly praising the other's deeds, rejoicing at each other's good success: but at parting, they fell to hot words together, Pompey upbraiding Lucullus' avarice, and Lucullus Pompey's ambition; so that their friends had much **ado** to part them.

Lucullus departing thence, divided the lands in Galatia which he had conquered; and bestowed them, and other gifts, on such as he thought good. Pompey, on the other side, camping near him, specially commanded the people in every part to obey him in nothing whatsoever he did: and besides, he took all his soldiers from him, leaving him only sixteen hundred, which he supposed were such, as for **disdain** and ill will they bare him, would do him but small service. Furthermore, to blemish the glory of his doings, he told everybody Lucullus had fought with the pomp and shadow only of these two kings, and that he had left him to fight with all their whole force and power, **Mithridates** being then prepared for wars, with shields, swords, and horses.

Lucullus, for revenge on the other side, said that Pompey went to fight but with a shadow of war; and that he was like a cowardly **buzzard** that preyeth upon dead bodies, which others have slain.

[Footnote: The Roman writer Pliny said that, on the other hand, Pompey called Lucullus "Xerxes in a toga."]

Narration and Discussion

Why were the Senators at first reluctant to offer Pompey such a powerful new command? Why was the proposal finally passed?

How did Pompey's actions show that he was not really as reluctant as he pretended to be?

Describe the "friendly meeting" between Pompey and Lucullus. (Christian students might consider 1 Corinthians 3:8-10; 22-23.)

Lesson Eleven

Introduction

The war against Mithridates and Tigranes finally came to an end.

Vocabulary

forthwith: immediately

choice of his army: best soldiers

impotent: weak

no shift: no other choice

embased: lowered, humiliated

Word Trivia

minas, talents: units of money. Other money words used later in the story: **miriades, drachmas**.

People

Hypsicratea: the sixth wife of Mithridates

Historic Occasions

66 B.C.: Lucullus returned to Rome, but was initially refused a triumph, and was allowed only limited involvement in state matters.

66 B.C.: Mithridates defeated at the **Battle of the Lycus**

66 B.C.: Surrender of Tigranes

On the Map

Phoenicia: a kingdom which had flourished in ancient times, but which had declined in power and which was now part of **Syria**

Bosporus: or **Bosphorus.** Now part of Turkey.

Euphrates River: a major river in the Middle East

Colchis: a region on the coast of the Black Sea; the legendary destination of the Argonauts

Sophene: a region of Armenia

Reading

Part One

Lucullus being now gone on his way, Pompey placed his whole navy in guard upon the sea, from the province of **Phoenicia** unto the realm of **Bosporus**. That done, he took his journey by land towards Mithridates; who had in his camp thirty thousand footmen, and two thousand horsemen, and yet durst not offer battle, but camped first upon a mountain of great strength, and hard to get up on: notwithstanding shortly after, he forsook it for lack of water. He was no sooner gone thence, but **forthwith** Pompey took it. Who, conjecturing by the nature of the plants and trees in that place which were very green, and also by divers holes he found, for that reason thereabouts should be some springs: he commanded them to dig wells in every corner, so that in a very short time all his camp had water enough; and he wondered at Mithridates, that he could not find that out in all the time he lay there.

In the end, he went and camped round about Mithridates, and entrenched him with a wall within his own camp: who, after he had abidden the siege five and forty days, fled away with all the **choice of his army**, unknown to Pompey; having first slain all the sick and **impotent** persons within his camp. After that, Pompey found him another time by the **Euphrates River**, and went and lodged hard by him. But fearing that Mithridates would pass over the river before he could prevent him in time, he raised his camp again, and marched away at midnight.

Part Two

[omission for length: Mithridates dreamed about being on a sinking ship]

As Mithridates was troubled with his ill-favoured dream, certain of his familiars came to him and told him that Pompey was come so near, that there was **no shift** but they must needs fight to defend their camp. Thereupon, his captains straight began to put his men in battle array, ready to fight. Pompey understanding they prepared to make defense, was in doubt to venture his men to fight in the dark, thinking it better to compass the enemy in to keep them from fleeing, and then in the morning to set upon them more easily, his men being the better soldiers. But Pompey's old captains were so earnestly in hand with him to persuade him they might fight, that in the end he was contented they should give charge.

Now it was not so dark but they could somewhat see, for the moon that was very low and. upon her setting, gave light enough to discern the body of a man: yet because the moon was very low, the shadow which gave out further far than their bodies, came almost even to their very enemies, which did let them that they could not certainly judge what space of ground was between them, but imagining that they were hard by them, they cast their darts at the Romans, but they hurt never a man, for their bodies were a great way from them.

The Romans perceiving that, ran upon them with great cries. But the barbarous people durst not abide their charge, they were so afraid; but turned their backs, and ran away for life, so that they were slain down right. Thus were there ten thousand of the barbarous people slain and more, and their camp also taken.

As for Mithridates himself, he at the beginning of the onset, with a body of eight hundred horse, charged through the Roman army, and made his escape. But before long all the rest dispersed, some one way, some another; and he was left only with three persons only, whereof **Hypsicratea** was one of the number, which had ever been valiant and had a man's heart: whereupon for that cause Mithridates called her "Hypsicrates." She at that time being arrayed like a man-of-arms of Persia, and mounted also on a horse after the Persian manner, was never weary with any long journey the king made, nor never left to wait upon his person, and to look to his horse: until such time as the king came to a strong castle called Inora, where was great store of gold and silver, and the king's chiefest treasure. Then Mithridates took of his richest apparel he had there, and gave it amongst them that were about him at that time, and a deadly poison besides to every one of his friends to carry about them, because they should not (unless they would themselves) fall into their enemies' hands alive.

From thence he thought to take his journey into Armenia, unto King Tigranes. Howbeit Tigranes sent to prevent him; and further proclaimed by trumpet, that he would give a hundred talents to anyone that could kill him. Thereupon, passing by the head of the river of Euphrates, Mithridates fled through the country of **Colchis**.

Part Three

In the meantime, Pompey invaded the country of Armenia, at the request of Tigranes the Younger, who had revolted against his father, and who went to meet with Pompey at the River of Araxes, which hath its beginning almost about the head of the Euphrates: but it runneth towards the east, and falleth into the Caspian Sea.

So they both together marched on further into the country, receiving such towns as yielded unto them. But King Tigranes (that not long before had been consumed and destroyed by Lucullus) understanding that Pompey was of a mild and gentle nature, he admitted Roman troops into his strongest forts and royal houses, and went himself with his friends and kinsmen to meet Pompey, and to yield himself unto him. When he came near to his camp, being a-horseback, there came out two sergeants of Pompey's, who commanded him to alight and go in afoot, for there was never man seen a-horseback within the Romans' camp. Tigranes did not only obey them, but further plucked off his sword and gave it them: and in fine, when he came almost to Pompey, taking of his royal hat from his head, he would have laid it at Pompey's feet, and falling down most shamefully on the ground, **embased** himself to embrace Pompey's knees. But Pompey himself prevented him, and taking him by the hand, made him to sit down by him on the one side of him, and his son on the other. Then he said unto them both: "As for the other losses you have sustained heretofore, you must thank Lucullus for them, who hath taken from you Syria, Phoenicia, Cilicia, Galatia, and Sophene; but for that you have left you till my coming, I will let you enjoy it, paying to the Romans a fine of six thousand talents for the injury you had done them; provided also that your son have the kingdom of **Sophene** for his part."

Tigranes accepted the conditions of peace. The Romans then saluted him king. He was so glad thereof that he promised to give every soldier half a **mina**, to every centurion ten minas, and to every colonel of a thousand men, a **talent**. His son was very angry withal: insomuch as Pompey sending for him to come to supper to him, he answered again, that was not the friendship he looked for at Pompey's hands, for he should find many other Romans that would offer him that courtesy. Pompey, for his answer, clapped him up as a prisoner, and kept him to be led in triumph at Rome.

[omission for length: Pompey's other victories in that region]

Narration and Discussion

Contrast the reactions of Tigranes and his son over surrendering to the Romans. Do you think one or the other showed more honour?

For older students or further study: Tigranes had another son, **Artavasdes II** (or **Artabazes**), who reigned in Armenia from 55 to 34 B.C., and who appears several times in the *Life of Crassus*. He has been contrasted in character to his brother Tigranes the Younger. What else can you find out about him?

Lesson Twelve and Examination Questions

Introduction

After claiming additional territory for the empire (including Judea), and attempting to settle disputes in those places, Pompey prepared to return to Italy himself. Some feared that he would enter Rome with an army and establish himself as dictator. He sent his soldiers home, however, with a reminder: "Come back for the triumph."

Vocabulary

in the flank: Dryden says "into the joints of his breastplate."

arbitration: working out terms of agreement between those having conflict. One who manages such negotiations is an **arbitrator**.

importunate: persistent (see **Lesson Five**)

Word Trivia

turves: also spelled **turfs**. These are cut-out sections of earth and vegetation, which could be piled up to stand on, or even used to build a wall (such as the early versions of Hadrian's Wall).

People

Oroeses: king of the Caucasian Albanians

Afranius: Lucius Afranius, who had served in Pompey's army, and was elected consul for the year 60 B.C. (probably due to bribes).

King Aristobulus: Aristobulus II, Jewish High Priest and King of Judea from 66 B.C. to 63 B.C.; the younger brother of **Hyrcanus II**, who had become king in 67 B.C. but surrendered to **Aristobulus** after a civil war. This did not end the strife in Judea, however, and allies of Hyrcanus besieged Jerusalem for months. Pompey's deputy in that region, **Marcus Aemilius Scaurus**, was offered (and may have accepted) bribes to help Aristobulus hold on to the throne; but when the matter came before Pompey, he decided in favour of Hyrcanus (perhaps seeing him as weaker and more likely to cooperate with Rome). Aristobulus was imprisoned, but later escaped and led an insurrection against Rome. He died by suicide in 49 B.C.

Scaurus: See above. As a footnote, it seems that money was an ongoing temptation for him; and in later life he was exiled from Rome as punishment for taking bribes. (He also married Pompey's former wife Mucia.)

Historic Occasions

65 B.C.: Phoenicia became part of the new Roman province of **Syria**

63 B.C.: Judea captured by Rome after the **Siege of Jerusalem**

63 B.C.: death of Mithridates

On the Map

Maeotian Sea: now called the Sea of Azov; connected to the Black Sea by the Strait of Kerch

Cyrnus River: or Cyrus; now called the Kura. It runs through Turkey, Georgia, and Azerbaijan.

Judea: the southern part of Palestine. You will also want to locate **Syria**.

Petra: a historic city in southern Jordan

Reading

Part One

The pursuit of Mithridates, who had thrown himself among the tribes inhabiting Bosporus and the shores of the **Maeotian Sea**, presented great difficulties. Furthermore also, he had news that the Albanians were rebelled again, which drew him back to be revenged of them. Thereupon he passed again over the **Cyrnus River**, with great pain and danger, because the barbarous people had made a strong defense a great way along the riverside, with a marvellous number of great trees, felled and laid across one over another. Furthermore, when he had with great difficulty passed through them, he fell into an evil-favoured country, where he should travel a great way before he could come to any water. Thereupon he caused ten thousand goatskins to be filled with water, and so went forward to meet with his enemies : being six score thousand footmen, and twelve thousand horsemen, but all (or the most of them) ill armed with wild beasts' skins. Their chieftain was a brother of **Oroeses** named Cosis. He, when the battle was begun, flew upon Pompey, and threw a dart at him, and hurt him **in the flank**. Pompey on the other side, ran Cosis through with his lance on both sides, and slew him stark dead.

[omission for length/content]

Part Two

He had a wonderful great desire to win **Syria**, and to go through the country of Arabia, even unto the Red Sea, specially because he saw Mithridates so ill to follow, and worse to overcome by force when he fled, than when he fought any battle; and that made him say that he would leave a sharper enemy behind him than himself (and by that he meant famine).

[omission for length]

Pompey now having by **Afranius** subdued the Arabians dwelling about Mount Amanus, he went himself in person into Syria, and made a government and province of it, being won to the Roman empire, for that it lacked a lawful king; and he conquered all **Judea** also, where he took **King Aristobulus**; and built certain cities there, and delivered others also from bondage, which by tyrants were forcibly kept, whom he chastised well enough. Howbeit he spent the most part of his time there deciding controversies, pacifying contentions and quarrels by **arbitration**, which fell out betwixt the free cities, princes and kings; and sent of his friends into those places where he could not come himself.

[omission for content]

Part Three

Now, the king of the Arabians, that dwelt about the castle called **Petra**, having never until that time made any account of the Roman army, was then greatly afraid of them, and wrote unto Pompey that he was at his devotion, to do what he would command him. Pompey thereupon to prove him, whether he meant as he spoke: brought his army before this castle of Petra. Howbeit this voyage was not liked of many men, because they saw it as an excuse to stop following Mithridates, against whom they would have preferred Pompey to use his force, being an ancient enemy to Rome; and that began to gather strength again, and prepared (as they heard say) to lead a great army through Scythia and Pannonia into Italy. But Pompey thinking he should sooner diminish Mithridates' power by suffering him to go on with wars, than that he should otherwise be able to take him flying: would not toil to follow him in vain. And for these causes he would needs make wars in other places, and linger time so long, that in the end he was put by his hope.

When he was not far from Petra, and had lodged his camp for that day: as he was riding and managing his horse up and down the camp, posts came flinging to him from the realm of Pontus, and brought him good news, as was easily to be discerned afar off by the heads of their javelins, which were wreathed about with laurel boughs. The soldiers, perceiving that, flocked straight about him; but Pompey would make an end of his riding first, before he read these letters. Howbeit they crying to him, and being **importunate** with him, he lighted from his horse, and returned into his camp, where there was no stone high enough for him to stand upon to speak unto them, and again, the soldiers would not tarry the making of one after the manner of their camp, which men of war do make themselves, with great **turves** of earth, laying one of them upon another: but for haste and earnest desire they had to hear what news there was in the letters, they laid together a heap of saddles one upon another, and Pompey getting up on them, told how Mithridates was dead, and had killed himself with his own hands, because his son Pharnaces did rebel against him, and had won all that which his father possessed: writing unto him that he "kept it for himself and the Romans."

Upon this news, all the camp ye may imagine, made wonderful joy, and did sacrifice to the gods, giving them thanks, and were as merry, as if in Mithridates' person alone, there had died an infinite number of their enemies.

Pompey by this occasion, having brought this war more easily to pass than he hoped for, departed presently out of Arabia, and having speedily in few days passed through the countries lying by the way, he came at length to the city of Amisus. There he found great presents that were brought unto him from Pharnaces, and many dead bodies of the king's blood, and amongst the rest, Mithridates' corpse. Pompey having ordered all things and established that province, went on his journey homewards with great pomp and glory.

[omission for length and content]

Part Four

So he thought at his return home into Italy, to have been very honourably received; and he longed to be at home, to see his wife and children, thinking also that they long looked for him; but the god that hath the charge given him, to mingle Fortune's prosperity with some bitter sop of adversity, laid a block in his way at home in his own house, to make his return more sorrowful.

[omission: the end of Pompey's marriage to Mucia]

Furthermore, there were rumours run abroad in Rome which troubled them sore, being given out that he would bring his army straight to Rome, and make himself absolute lord of all the Roman empire. Crassus thereupon, either for that he believed it indeed to be true, or (as it was thought) to make the accusation true, and the envy towards Pompey the greater: conveyed himself, his family, and goods, suddenly out of Rome.

So Pompey when he came into Italy, called all his soldiers together, and after he had made an oration unto them, as time and occasion required, he commanded them to sever themselves, and every man to repair home to apply his business (remembering to meet at Rome together at the day of his triumph). His army being thus dispersed, and straight reported abroad for news: a marvellous thing happened unto him. The cities seeing Pompey the Great without soldiers, having but a small train about him of his familiar friends only: they went all of them to meet him, not as though he were returned home from his great conquests, but from some journey taken for his pleasure. Such was the love of the people to him that they accompanied him to Rome, whether he would or not, with a greater power than that he had brought into Italy: so that if he had been disposed to have made any innovation in the commonwealth, he had not needed his army.

Narration and Discussion

How was Pompey's return to Rome both worse and better than he expected?

For older students: In an omitted passage, Plutarch makes this comment: "If Pompey's fame and renown were great, no less was his virtue, justice, and liberality, which indeed did hide many faults his friends and familiars about him did commit. For truly he was of so gentle a nature, that he could neither keep them from offending, nor yet punish them when they had offended. Notwithstanding, he did use them so well that complained unto him, or that had to deal with him in any matter, that he made them contented patiently to bear their covetousness and straight dealing." Pompey's general reputation in war and politics might not seem to agree with calling him "gentle," yet

Plutarch makes the point that, with those he called friends, he could forgive much—even, perhaps, overmuch. When is it a virtue to "hide" the faults or sins of others, and when is it dishonest or conniving? See Proverbs 10:12, 12:22-23, and 17:9.

For older students or further study: What can you find out about the **Siege of Jerusalem**?

Examination Questions for Part One

Younger Students:

1. "Pompey was for many occasions beloved." Describe two of the reasons he was beloved (or admired). Also, tell anything you know about his personal appearance.

Older Students:

1. Describe the occasion when Pompey and Sulla each saluted the other as "Imperator." How did Pompey later make an enemy of Sulla?
2. (For high school) Why did the Romans make Pompey general by sea? Describe the scene that followed the decree, and Pompey's treatment of the pirates.

Lesson 13

Introduction

This lesson describes Pompey's third triumph in some detail. It also introduces a more questionable side of Pompey's character: his willingness to commit bribery on others' behalf.

Vocabulary

defer: postpone

prefer: propose, support

certain money: that is, bribes

would have served…: Pompey had enough armour, treasure, and prisoners to have continued longer than the two days allotted.

tables: large placards or signs

replenishment: Dryden says Pompey "founded" these towns, but North says he "replenished" them, by settling people there

sundry: various

under four-and-thirty years of age: Alexander the Great died at 32 years of age. Plutarch says that Pompey was almost 40 at this time; but, according to his birthdate of 106 B.C., he was closer to 45.

People

Piso (#2): Marcus Pupius Piso Frugi Calpurnianus, Pompey's lieutenant

Cato: Marcus Porcius Cato Uticensis, the subject of Plutarch's *Life of Cato the Younger*; a statesman known for his moral integrity

Afranius: see **Lesson Twelve**

Commagenians: those of the Armenian kingdom of Commagene

Historic Occasions

63 B.C.: Lucullus had his long-delayed triumph in Rome

61 B.C.: Piso (#2) was consul

61 B.C.: Pompey's third triumph

On the Map

As you begin the second half of the study, you may wish to review some of the places mentioned previously. This lesson provides an extra opportunity by listing many places which became part of the Roman empire. How many can you find on a map?

Reading

Part One

In those days there was a law that no man should enter into Rome before his triumph: whereupon Pompey sent to the Senate, to pray them to **defer** the choosing of consuls for a few days, because he might be present to support **Piso (#2)**, who sued for the consulship that year. They denied him his request, by **Cato's** means that hindered it. Pompey, marvelling to hear of Cato's boldness and plain speech, had a marvellous desire to win him, and to make him his friend. So Cato having two nieces, Pompey desired to marry the one himself, and take the other for his son. But Cato, mistrusting this desire of Pompey's and believing that it was a scheme only to win and corrupt him: denied him flatly. His wife and sister, on the other side, were angry with him for refusing to make alliance with Pompey the Great.

About that time it chanced that Pompey, being very desirous to **prefer Afranius** to be consul, gave a sum of money among the tribes for their votes, and people came and received it in his own gardens. This thing being reported abroad in the city, every man spoke ill of Pompey: that he put the consulship to sale for money, unto those that could not deserve it by virtue; since he himself only had obtained it by "purchase," by many a noble and worthy deed.

Then said Cato to his wife and sister: "Lo now, we would have been partakers of this fault too, had we matched with Pompey." When they heard it, they confessed he had reason to refuse the match, for equity and his honour.

Part Two

But now to Pompey's triumph. For the stateliness and magnificence thereof, although he had two days' space to show it, yet he lacked time: for there were many things prepared for the show, that were not seen, which **would have served to have set out another triumph**.

First there were **tables** carried, whereon were written the names and titles of all the people and nations for the which he triumphed, as these that follow. The kingdoms of Pontus, Armenia, Cappadocia, Paphlagonia, Media, Colchis, Iberia, Albania, Syria, Cilicia, and Mesopotamia; and furthermore, the people that dwell about Phoenicia and Palestine, Judea, and Arabia: and all the pirates which he had overcome both by sea and by land, in all parts of the world. And in these different countries there appeared the capture of no less than one thousand fortified places, nor much less than nine hundred cities, together with eight hundred ships of the pirates, and the **replenishment** of thirty-nine towns.

Moreover, these tables declared that the revenue of the commonwealth of Rome, before these conquests he made, amounted yearly but to five thousand miriades; and that from thenceforth with the sums he had added unto the former revenue, they should now receive eight thousand and five hundred miriades: and that he brought presently in ready gold and silver, and in plate and jewels, to put into the common treasury, the value of twenty thousand talents, besides that which had been distributed already amongst the soldiers: of the which, he that had left for his share, had fifteen hundred drachmas.

The prisoners that were led in the show of this triumph, besides the captains of the pirates, were these that follow: the son of Tigranes, King of Armenia, with his wife and daughter; the wife of king Tigranes himself, called Zosime; Aristobulus, King of Judea; Mithridates' sister, with five sons of hers; and some ladies of Scythia; the hostages also of the Iberians and the Albanians, and also of the kings of the **Commagenians**; over and besides a great number of other marks of triumphs which himself or his lieutenants had won at **sundry** battles in divers places.

But the greatest honour that ever he won, and which never any other consul of the Romans but himself obtained, was this: that he made his third triumph of the three parts of the world. Divers other Romans had triumphed thrice before him: howbeit, he first triumphed of Africa, the second time of Europe, the third time of Asia. So that it appeared by these three triumphs that he had triumphed in manner of all the land that is inhabited, being at that time (as it is reported by them which compare his doings unto Alexander the Great) **under four-and-thirty years of age** (though in truth at that time he was near forty). O, happy would it have been for him if he had died when he had Alexander's fortune: for all his life afterwards made his prosperity hateful, or his adversity miserable. Employing the honour and authority he had gotten by his valiantness, favouring men's unjust causes: the more he furthered them, the more he lessened his honour, and unawares brought his greatness to nothing.

For like as when the strongest places of a city, which receiving their enemies into them, do give them the benefit of their own strength: even so, through Pompey's power, Caesar, growing to be great, overthrew him in the end with the selfsame means he employed to the overthrow of others. And thus it fortuned.

Narration and Discussion

Pompey might have justified bribery as generosity and friendship. Cato obviously didn't agree. Which side would you have taken?

For older students: "O, happy would it have been for him if he had died…" Is Plutarch's reason for saying this clear yet, or is it something to consider as the second half of the story unfolds?

Lesson 14

Introduction

Lucullus, although he had returned to Rome somewhat in disgrace, had nevertheless come back with a great deal of wealth, and had eventually been granted his triumph. He also seemed to have regained some support in the Senate, especially from those who did not care for Pompey.

Vocabulary

uncourteously used him: treated him disrespectfully

finding he had such a repulse...: Pompey was getting little support from the senators, so he turned to others such as the tribunes

recompense: reward

in danger of law: Cicero was accused of putting conspirators to death without a proper trial.

sue for his first consulship: Caesar was elected consul for 59 B.C., along with **Bibulus**

pestilent device: nasty scheme

subtle practice: sneaky trick

lowering the dignity...: It was not so much that the consul (or chief magistrate) could not perform a compassionate act, but rather that others (such as tribunes) were responsible for such matters.

upon the hustings: before the people

approbation: approval, agreement

buckler: Dryden's word for shield

affianced, or made sure before: engaged, betrothed

People

Clodius: Publius Clodius Pulcher. The long-running strife between Clodius and **Cicero** is described in the *Life of Cicero*.

Cicero: Marcus Tullius Cicero, an orator who was the subject of Plutarch's *Life of Cicero*

Bibulus: Marcus Calpurnius Bibulus

Historic Occasions

60 B.C.: Caesar's return to Rome

60 or 59 B.C. to 53 B.C.: First Triumvirate, an alliance between Pompey, Julius Caesar, and Crassus

59 B.C.: Julius Caesar was consul (with Bibulus)

59 B.C.: Pompey married **Julia** (fourth wife)

58-57 B.C.: Exile of Cicero

Reading

Part One

Lucullus, at his return out of Asia (where Pompey had **uncourteously used him**) was then very well taken of the Senate, and much more when Pompey was also come to Rome. For the Senate did counsel and encourage him to deal in the affairs of the state, seeing him given too much to his ease and pleasure, by reason of his great wealth he had gotten. So when Pompey was come, he (Lucullus) began to speak against him, and through the friendship and assistance of Cato, confirmed all his doings in Asia which Pompey had broken and rejected.

Pompey, **finding he had such a repulse of the Senate**, was driven to have recourse unto the tribunes of the people, and to fall in friendship with light young men. Of the tribunes, the most impudent and vilest person was **Clodius**: who received him, and made him a prey unto the people. For he had Pompey ever at his elbow, and against his honour carried him up and down the Forum after him, to speak as the occasion served to confirm any matter or device which he preferred unto him to flatter the common people. And further, for **recompense** of his goodwill, he craved of Pompey (not as a thing dishonourable, but beneficial for him) that he would forsake **Cicero**, who was his friend, and had done much for him in matters of commonwealth. Pompey granted his request. Thereupon Cicero being brought **in danger of law**, and requiring Pompey's friendship to help him, Pompey shut his door against them that came to speak in his behalf, and went out himself at another back door. Cicero thereupon, fearing the extremity of law, willingly forsook Rome.

Part Two

At that time, **Julius Caesar** returning home from his praetorship out of Spain, began to lay such a plot that presently brought him into great favour, and afterwards much increased his power, but otherwise utterly undid Pompey and the commonwealth.

Now he was to **sue for his first consulship**, and considering the enmity betwixt Pompey and Crassus: if he joined with the one, he made the other his enemy: so he devised to make them friends, a thing seeming of great honesty at the first sight, but yet a **pestilent device**, and as **subtle** a **practice** as could be. For he well knew that opposite parties or factions in a commonwealth, like passengers in a boat, serve to trim and balance the unsteady motions of power there; whereas if they combine and come all over to one side, they cause a shock which will be sure to overset the vessel and carry down everything.

Whereupon, Cato wisely told them afterwards that the civil wars betwixt Pompey and Caesar had caused the destruction of the commonwealth; but that their enmity and discord was not the chief original cause of this misery, but rather their friendship and agreement.

Part Three

Caesar, being thus elected consul, began at once to make an interest with the poor and meaner sort, by preferring and establishing laws for planting colonies and dividing lands, **lowering the dignity of his**

office, and turning his consulship into a sort of tribuneship rather. And when Bibulus, his colleague, opposed him (and Cato was prepared to second Bibulus, and assist him vigorously); Caesar brought Pompey **upon the hustings**, and addressing him in the sight of the people, demanded his opinion upon the laws that were proposed. Pompey gave his **approbation**. "Then," said Caesar, "in case any man should offer violence to these laws, will you be ready to give assistance to the people?" "Yes," replied Pompey, "I shall be ready, and against those that threaten the sword, I will appear with sword and **buckler**."

Pompey in all his life never did nor spoke anything that men more misliked, than that which he said at that time. His friends excused him, and said it was a word passed his mouth before he was aware: but his deeds afterwards showed, that he was altogether at Caesar's commandment. For not many days after, he married Julia the daughter of Caesar, which was **affianced, or made sure before**, unto Servilius Caepio when no man thought of it; and to pacify Caepio's anger, he gave him his own daughter in marriage, whom he had also promised before unto Faustus the son of Sulla; and Caesar also married Calpurnia, the daughter of Piso (#3).

Narration and Discussion

How did Pompey's previous treatment of Lucullus come back against him now?

The theme of friendship (genuine or contrived, positive or negative) runs through this lesson. For example:

> The condition of Pompey's new friendship with Clodius was that he had to end his old friendship with Cicero. Have you ever been in such a situation? What would you do?

> Why did Caesar want to make peace between Pompey and Crassus?

> Cato later said that "the enmity and discord between Pompey and Caesar was not the chief original cause of this misery the civil war in Rome, but rather their friendship..." What did he mean?

Lesson 15

Introduction

Pompey was now one of the most powerful men in Rome: perhaps by his own merit, or perhaps because he had attached himself to the rising star of Julius Caesar. Plutarch says later that Pompey grew to have "pride and a glorious conceit of himself." At this time, however, he received a sharp reminder that not everyone felt the same way.

Vocabulary

taken with this bait: pleased with the generous land grants

bills: written statements to hand out or post publicly

lay still and took his pleasure: retired and relaxed (see **Lesson Seven**)

doted of: in love with

seditious attempts: uprisings

had sent away Cato to make wars in Cyprus: This story is told in the *Life of Cato the Younger.*.

pretense: excuse

a warm dispute: a heated battle

Word Trivia

dissolute: immoral, without principle. It is related to the word "dissolve," and comes from words meaning "disconnected, loose." Without solid principles, morals have nothing to stick themselves to.

People

Piso (#3): Lucius Calpurnius Piso Caesoninus, consul in 58 B.C.

Gabinius: see **Lesson Eight**

Historic Occasions

58 B.C.: Rome acquired the country of **Cyprus**; Cato was sent there to negotiate, but mostly to get him out of the way

On the Map

Julius Caesar was made the governor of **Gaul** and **Illyria**. Illyria is the region on the eastern side of the Adriatic Sea, north of Greece and west of Macedon. (If you are using Constable's *Historical Atlas of Ancient Rome*, look at the maps on pages 55 and 75.)

Cyprus: an island country in the eastern Mediterranean Sea, which had been conquered by Alexander the Great and then claimed by the rulers of Egypt, before becoming part of the Roman empire.

Reading

Part One

After this, Pompey, filling all Rome with soldiers, did what he would by force. For as the consul Bibulus came into the Forum accompanied with Lucullus and Cato, they suddenly set upon him, and broke the bundles of rods which his officers carried before him; and someone, whatsoever he was, cast a basket of horse dung upon his head. Moreover, the two tribunes that were in his company were also very sore hurt. By this means, having cleared the Forum of all their enemies, they passed the law for division of lands, as they wished it themselves. The people being **taken with this bait**, were contented to be ruled by them as they would; and would never stick at any matter that they would have passed. So were all Pompey's matters confirmed, which Lucullus was against; and they appointed unto Caesar also the government of the **Gauls** on this side and beyond the Alps; and **Illyria** for five years' space, with four whole legions.

The next year following were appointed as consuls Piso (#3), Caesar's father-in-law; and **Gabinius**, the greatest flatterer Pompey had about him. But for now, while things stood in these terms, Bibulus, though he were consul, kept himself close in his house for eight months' space, and only sent out **bills**, and set them up on every post in open places, accusing Pompey and Caesar. Cato, on the other side, as if he had been inspired with the spirit of prophecy, told openly in the Senate house what would become of the commonwealth and Pompey.

Lucullus growing old, **lay still and took his pleasure**, and would no more meddle in the commonwealth. At that time it was that Pompey said that it was more unseasonable for an old man to follow his pleasure than to attend matters of the commonwealth. Yet he himself shortly after was so **doted of** his young wife, that he would follow her up and down in the country, and in his gardens, and leave all affairs of weight aside.

Part Two

Whereupon Clodius, being then tribune of the people, despised Pompey, and began to enter into **seditious attempts**. For when he had driven Cicero out of Rome, and **had sent away Cato to make wars in Cyprus** (Caesar was likewise occupied in Gaul); and finding that the people in like case were at his commandment, because to flatter them he did what they would have him: he attempted to undo some things that Pompey had established. Amongst other things, he took King Tigranes out of prison, and ever carried him up and down with him wheresoever he went; and continually picked quarrels unto Pompey's friends, to try what credit he had.

In the end, Pompey coming abroad one day into the common assembly, to hear how a matter of his was handled: this Clodius having a company of vagabonds and desperate men about him, that cared not what they did: he sitting in a place where he might be seen from the rest, began to ask rude questions out aloud, such as "Who is the **dissolute** general?" They, like a company of dancers or singers, when he spoke and clapped his hands on his gown, answered him straight aloud to every question, that it was "Pompey." This went to Pompey's heart, that was not wont to hear himself so ill spoken of openly, neither was acquainted with any such kind of sight: but yet it made him bite the lip more, when he saw the Senate glad to see him thus shamed and reproved, as a just revenge and punishment for his vile betraying and forsaking of Cicero.

So, great stir and uproar being made upon this in the Forum, and many men sore hurt; and one of Clodius' bondmen being taken also in the press of the people with a sword in his hand, very near unto Pompey: Pompey laid hold of this **pretense**, though perhaps otherwise apprehensive of Clodius' insolence and bad language, and he would never after come into the Forum, as long as Clodius was tribune; but kept at home still, consulting with his friends what way he should take to appease the anger of the Senate against him.

Thereupon, one of his friends, called Culleo, advised him to put away his wife Julia, and utterly to refuse Caesar's friendship to gain that of the Senate: this he would not hearken to. Notwithstanding he was contented to hearken unto them that gave him counsel to call Cicero home again, who was Clodius' mortal enemy, and in great favour with the Senate. Thereupon, he brought Cicero's brother into the Forum, to move the matter to the people: where, after **a warm dispute**, in which several were wounded and some slain, he got the victory over Clodius.

Narration and Discussion

Why did Bibulus spend most of the year hiding in his house?

What happened to Pompey's friendship with Clodius?

For older students: It is said that "power corrupts." Is it possible for anyone to use great power prudently?

Lesson 16

Introduction

At this time Rome was experiencing severe grain shortages, which caused people (especially the poorer ones) to be unhappy with the government. Cicero, newly returned from exile, proposed making Pompey the person to oversee the food supply, which would mean traveling to places like Sardinia, Sicily, and Africa to bring back grain.

That suggestion was met with two different negative responses: some said that the whole shortage was just an invention to increase Pompey's popularity, which seemed to be slipping; others suggested that it was just a way to keep him busy so that he wouldn't involve himself in Egyptian issues. However, the motion passed, and Pompey's mission was successful.

But that was only the beginning of many power-seeking games in Rome.

Vocabulary

corn: grain, such as wheat or barley

trade of merchandise and tillage: agriculture and grocery business

into his kingdom: see note about **King Ptolemy**

cast it out: refused to pass the motion; threw it out

hazard his person: risk his safety

set him aloft: raise him to great power

Englishmen: the tribes living in what is now England

he did harden…: Caesar was training his troops for battle.

nothing the more…: that is, no more honestly or uprightly than the way in which they had become consuls in the first place

falsely alleging that he had noted certain ill signs: Pompey is said to have cried out that it was thundering (the Romans believed thunder to be a bad omen).

for five years more; authorizing Caesar's charge for five years longer: Why was Caesar so eager to prolong his time as governor? One practical reason is that while he held public office (such as consul or proconsul), he was immune from private lawsuits; but as soon as he stepped down (or became **private**), he would have to deal with them (and there were, apparently, a number of them).

peradventure: perhaps

cast (him) in the teeth: upbraid or reproach

not to desist: not to back down from the race

charge: territory for which he was responsible

Word Trivia

specious: misleading, especially misleadingly attractive; appearing to be true but not really so. Its roots come from words meaning "fair" or "beautiful." We see this idea used in the expression "a pretty argument," which is not to be confused with "a petty argument."

People

Lentulus Spinther: consul for 57 B.C.

King Ptolemy of Egypt: Sometimes spelled Ptolomy. **Ptolemy XII** reigned 80-58 and 55-51 B.C. (Between 58-55 B.C., he was exiled in Rome.) After his death, his son **Ptolemy XIII reigned** from 51-47 B.C., along with Cleopatra (sister of Ptolemy XIII).

Domitius (#2): consul in 54 B.C.; the brother-in-law of Cato

Historic Occasions

58 B.C.: Pompey chosen to remedy grain shortages

56 B.C.: Caesar, Crassus, and Pompey met at **Luca**

56 B.C.: Pompey's fiftieth birthday

55 B.C.: Pompey's second consulship (with Crassus)

On the Map

Luca: The southernmost town in Cisalpine Gaul (or northern Italy); now spelled **Lucca**.

Parthia: a region of ancient Iran, known for its military strength

Reading

Part One

No sooner was Cicero returned home upon this decree, but immediately he used his efforts to reconcile the Senate to Pompey; and by speaking in favour of the law upon the importations of **corn**, did again, in effect, make Pompey sovereign lord of all the Roman possessions by sea and land. For all the havens, marts and fairs, and all storehouses for corn, yea moreover all the **trade of merchandise and tillage**, came under Pompey's hands. Then Clodius accusing him, said that the Senate had not made this law *because* of the scarcity of victuals, but that they *made* the scarcity of victuals; because the law should pass only to revive Pompey's power and authority again. Others say that this was a device of **Lentulus Spinther** the consul, who gave Pompey the greater authority, because he might be sent to put the elder **King Ptolemy** again **into his kingdom**.

This notwithstanding, Canidius the tribune proposed another law to send Pompey, without an army (with two sergeants only to carry the axes before him), to bring Ptolemy in favour again with the Alexandrians. Neither did this proposal seem unacceptable to Pompey, though the Senate **cast it out** upon the **specious** pretense that they were unwilling to **hazard his person**. Nevertheless, little papers were found thrown about the Forum and the Senate house, declaring that Ptolemy desired that Pompey might come to aid him instead of Spinther.

So, Pompey having now full authority to cause corn to be brought to Rome, he sent then his lieutenants and friends abroad, and he himself in person went into Sicily.

Now being ready to return again, there rose such a storm of wind in the sea, that the mariners were in doubt to weigh their anchors. But he himself first embarked, and commanded them straight to hoist sail, crying out aloud, "It is of necessity I must go, but not to live." So, through his boldness and good spirit, using the good fortune he had, he filled all the markets with corn, and all the sea besides with ships: insomuch, the plenty he brought did not only furnish the city of Rome; but all their neighbours also about them, and it came like a lively spring that dispersed itself through all Italy.

Part Two

About that time, the great conquests that Caesar made in Gaul did **set him aloft**. For when they thought that he was occupied in wars far from Rome (with the Belgians, Swiss, and **Englishmen**), he, by secret plotting, was in the midst among the people at Rome; and most against Pompey in the weightiest affairs of the commonwealth. For he had the power of an army about his person, which **he did harden with pains and continual practice**, not with intent to fight only against the barbarous people: for the battles he had with them were in manner but as a hunting sport, by the which he made himself invincible, and dreadful to the world. But furthermore, by the infinite gold and silver, and the incredible spoils and treasure which he won upon the enemies whom he had overcome; and by sending great presents also to Rome, to the aediles, praetors, consuls, and their wives, he purchased himself many friends.

Therefore, after he had passed over the Alps again, and was come to winter in the city of **Luca**: a world of people (both men and women), and of the Senate themselves almost two hundred persons (amongst them Crassus and Pompey), went out of Rome unto him. Furthermore, there were seen at Caesar's gate six score sergeants carrying axes before praetors, or proconsuls. So Caesar sent every one of them back again either full of money or good words: but with Pompey and Crassus, he made a match that they two together should sue to be consuls; and that he himself would send them good aid to Rome, at the day of election, to give their voices. And if they were chosen, that they should then practise, by decree of the people, to have the governments of some new provinces and armies assigned them: and withal, that they should confirm the government of those provinces he had himself, **for five years more**.

When these arrangements came to be generally known, great indignation was excited among the chief men in Rome. Whereupon **Marcellinus** at an open assembly of the people, did ask them both if they would sue for the consulship at the next election. So they being urged by the people to make answer, Pompey spoke first, and said: **peradventure** he would, peradventure not. Crassus answered more gently, that he would do that which should be best for the commonwealth. Then Marcellinus sharply inveighing against Pompey:

Pompey angrily again **cast him in the teeth**, and said that Marcellinus was the rankest churl, and the unthankfullest beast in the world: for that of a poorly-spoken man, he had made him eloquent, and being in manner starved and famished, many a time he had filled his belly.

This notwithstanding, divers that before were determined to sue for the consulship went no further in it. Cato alone persuaded and encouraged **Lucius Domitius (#2) not to desist**. "For," said he, "thou dost not contend for the consulship, but to defend the common liberty of thy country against two tyrants." Pompey therefore fearing Cato's party, lest that having all the Senate's goodwills, he should draw also the best part of the people after him: he thought it not good to suffer Domitius (#2) to come into the Forum. To this end therefore, he sent men armed against him, who at the first onset, slew the torchbearer that carried the torch before him, and made all the rest flee: amongst whom also Cato was the last man that retired, who was hurt in his elbow defending of Domitius.

Part Three

Pompey and Crassus having become consuls after this sort, they ordered themselves **nothing the more temperately, nor honestly**. For first of all, the people being about to choose Cato praetor: Pompey, being at the assembly of the election, perceiving that they would choose him, broke up the assembly, **falsely alleging that he had noted certain ill signs**; and afterwards, the tribes of the people being bribed and corrupted with money, they chose Antias and Vatinius praetors.

After that, by Trebonius, tribune of the people, they published edicts, **authorizing Caesar's charge for five years longer**, according to the agreement they had made with Caesar. Unto Crassus also they had appointed Syria, and the war against the **Parthians**. Unto Pompey in like case, all Africa, and both Spains, with four legions besides: of the which, at Caesar's desire, he lent him two legions to help him in his war in Gaul.

Narration and Discussion

In **Lesson One**, Plutarch said that the Romans hated Pompey's father for his greed, but that Pompey's character was quite different. Pompey may not have been greedy for money, but there were certain other things he was determined to have, at almost any cost. Can you explain?

What were some signs that Julius Caesar was readying himself to take control of Rome?

"When these arrangements came to be generally known, great indignation was excited among the chief men in Rome." How did Pompey and Crassus get away with dishonesty (and even violence)?

Creative narration: Expand on the conversation between Cato and Domitius, and the scene with the torchbearer. How might Shakespeare have dramatized this?

Lesson 17

Introduction

Pompey and Crassus had both been granted the government of overseas provinces; but while Crassus left to fight against the Parthians, Pompey remained in Rome to dedicate his Theatre and (to the annoyance of many) to spend time with his wife. However, this period of seeming good fortune quickly came to an end, as Pompey had to deal with both personal tragedy and the increasing power of his former Triumvirate ally, Julius Caesar.

Vocabulary

expiration: end

theatre: The Theatre of Pompey, the first permanent theatre to be built in Rome, was begun around 61 B.C. and completed in 55 B.C. The Theatre included a whole complex of buildings, including space used for political meetings. To get around "zoning" problems, Pompey had the complex built just over the city boundary line; and to further legitimize the project, he included a temple to Venus, and said that the theatre seats were steps leading up to the temple.

defrayed: paid for

continency: faithfulness

great with child: pregnant

was delivered: had the baby

death had put an end to that relation: Pompey and Caesar had been on good terms while Pompey was married to Julia; but now that she was gone, there was no motivation to continue the relationship.

covetousness: wanting to possess what one does not have. One of the Ten Commandments, in older English translations, says "Thou shalt not covet" (Exodus 20:17).

because the citizens that made the elections…: Ironically, Pompey was kept out of office because of the same bribery tactics he had previously used himself.

dictator: Rome was usually governed by two consuls, but in times of emergency one sole leader, called the dictator, could be appointed.

commended: praised

death of one of the consuls: Neither Domitius (#2) nor Messalla appears to have died in office, so it is not clear what is meant here. It may refer to the murder of **Clodius** at the hands of Milo, who was one of the candidates for consul.

consul alone: that is, without any co-consul

in respect of him that spoke it: considering how Bibulus had been mistreated while he was consul

Word Trivia

theatre: Our use of the word "theatre" (or "theater" in the U.S.) as mainly a place where plays (and now movies) are shown dates back only to Shakespeare's lifetime. The word comes from a Greek word meaning "something to see," in the same sense as the English term "a spectacle." The "spectacles" at Pompey's theatre included music, combat, and gymnastic events.

hurly-burly: hubbub or commotion. The first known use of **hurly-burly** was in 1539.

People

Domitius (#3) and Messalla: Gnaeus Domitius Calvinus and Marcus Valerius Messalla Rufus, consuls for 53 B.C. **Domitius (#3)** is described more fully in **Lesson 21**.

Historic Occasions

55 B.C.: dedication of Pompey's Theatre

54 B.C.: death of Pompey's wife Julia

53 B.C.: death of Crassus and his son at the Battle of Carrhae in Parthia

53 B.C.: Domitius and Messalla were consuls

52 B.C.: Pompey chosen as sole consul until reasonable order could be restored in Rome. He then partnered with **Metellus Scipio** (#2, see next lesson) for the rest of the year.

Reading

Part One

These things done, Crassus departed to his province, at the **expiration** of his consulship; and Pompey remained at Rome about the dedicating of his **theatre**, where he treated the people with all sorts of games, shows, in exercises, in gymnastics alike and in music. There was likewise the hunting or baiting of wild beasts, and combats with them, in which five hundred lions were slain; but above all, the battle of elephants was a spectacle full of horror and amazement. This great charge and bountiful expense, **defrayed** by Pompey, to show the people pastime and pleasure, made him again to be very much esteemed of and beloved amongst the people. But on the other side, he won himself as much ill-will and envy, in committing the government of his provinces and legions into the hands of his lieutenants, whilst he himself roamed up and down the pleasant places of Italy, with his wife at his pleasure: either because he was far in love with her, or else for that she loved him so dearly that he could not find in his heart to leave her company.

It was reported of her, (being known of many) that this young lady Julia loved her husband more dearly, not for Pompey's flourishing age, but for his assured **continency**, knowing no other woman but her: besides also, he was no solemn man, but pleasant of conversation, which made women love him marvellously. It is certain, that at an election of the aediles, men rising suddenly in **hurly-burly**, drew their swords, and many were slain about Pompey: insomuch as his clothes being bloodied, he sent his men home in haste to fetch him other to change him. His young wife that was **great with child**, seeing his clothes bloody, took such a flight upon it, that she fell down in a swoon before them, and they had much ado to recover her; and yet she fell straight in labour upon it, and **was delivered**. So that they themselves, which blamed him most for his good will he bare unto Caesar, could not reprove the love he bare unto his wife. Another time after that, she was great with child again, whereof she died; and the child lived not many days after the mother.

[omission for length]

Part Two

For the city now at once began to roll and swell, so to say, with the stir of the coming storm. Things everywhere were in a state of agitation, and everybody's discourse tended to division, now that **death had put an end to that relation** which hitherto had been a disguise rather than restraint to the ambition of these men. Not long after that also came news that Crassus was overthrown and slain in Parthia: he had been a safeguard to keep the two from civil wars, for that they both feared him, and therefore kept themselves in a reasonable sort together. But Fortune had taken away this third champion, who could have withstood the better of them both that had overcome the other. So little can Fortune prevail against nature, having no power to stop **covetousness**: since so large and great an empire, and such a wide country besides, could not contain the covetous desire of these two men. But though they had often both heard and read,

> "Among the gods themselves all things by
> lot divided are,
>
> And none of them intrudes himself within
> his neighbour's share, "

yet they thought not that the empire of Rome was enough for them, which were but two.

But Pompey spoke openly in an oration he made unto the people, that he ever came to office before he looked for it; and also left it sooner than they thought he would have done: and that he witnessed by discharging his army so soon. Then, thinking that Caesar would not discharge his army, he sought to make himself strong against him by procuring offices of the city, without any other alteration. Neither would he seem to mistrust him; but he plainly shewed that he did despise and contemn him. But when he saw that he could not obtain the offices of the city as he would, **because the citizens that made the elections were bribed with money**: he then left it without a magistrate, so that there was none either to command, or that the people should obey.

Hereupon there was mention straightway made of appointing a **dictator**. The first man that propounded it was Lucilius, tribune of the people, who persuaded them to choose Pompey. But Cato stuck so stoutly against it, that the tribune had like to have lost his office, even in the Forum. But then many of Pompey's friends stepped up, and excused him, saying that he neither sought, nor would have the dictatorship. Then Cato **commended** him much, and praying him to see good order kept in the commonwealth: Pompey being ashamed to deny so reasonable a request, was careful of it.

Thereupon two consuls were chosen, **Domitius and Messalla**.

But shortly afterwards, when the state began to change again by the **death of one of the consuls**; and that many were more earnestly bent to have a dictator than before; Cato, fearing it would break out with fury, determined to give Pompey some office of reasonable authority, to keep him from the other which would be more tyrannical. Insomuch, Bibulus himself being chief of the Senate, and Pompey's enemy, was the first that moved that Pompey might be chosen **consul alone**: for, said he, by this means, either the commonwealth shall be rid of the present trouble, or else it shall be in bondage to an honest man. This opinion was marvelled at, **in respect of him that spoke it**.

Whereupon, Cato standing up, it was thought straight he would have spoken against him. But silence being made him, he plainly told them, that for his own part he would not have been the first man to have propounded that which was spoken: but since it was spoken by another, that he thought it reasonable and meet to be followed. And therefore, said he, it is better to have an officer to command, whatsoever he be, rather than none: and that he saw no man fitter to command than Pompey, in so troublesome a time.

All the Senate liked his opinion, and ordained that Pompey should be chosen sole consul; and that if he saw, in his discretion, that he should need the assistance of another companion, he might name any whom he thought good, but not till two months were past. Thus was Pompey made consul alone (by Sulpitius, regent for that day).

Then Pompey made very friendly countenance unto Cato; and thanked him for the honour he had done him, praying him privately to assist him with his counsel in the consulship. Cato answered him, that there was no cause why he should thank him, for he had spoken nothing for his sake, but for respect of the commonwealth only: and for his counsel, if he would ask it, he should privately have it; if not, yet that he would openly say that which he thought. Such a man was Cato in all his doings.

Narration and Discussion

How was it that the Roman empire (the largest the world had ever seen) still did not seem large enough to contain the "covetous desires" of both Pompey and Caesar?

Why was it so surprising that Bibulus and Cato supported the idea of making Pompey sole consul? Why do you think they did so?

For older students: How was Cato the opposite of one with "covetous desires?" (Look up Proverbs 11:23; James 3:13.)

Lesson 18

Introduction

Pompey, now in his fifties, married a woman who was much younger but who seemed to be his equal in intellect. (We will hear more about her later.) On the political front, tensions were building with Julius Caesar; but Pompey, riding a wave of public affection after recovering from an illness, seemed oblivious to the idea that his time in power might be running out.

Vocabulary

maiden: unmarried woman

the remedy to redress the same: they expected Pompey (in Dryden's words, like a physician) to be the cure for their ills

disposed upon him against the law...: outside of the usual rule of having two consuls, because Rome was in a crisis state

let fall his suit: dropped the case

crave recompense: seek reward

nosegays: small bouquets

Word Trivia

private man: without any official (public) position, and (especially) without an army. Traced back to its first Latin roots, the word "private" (for one person, or owned by one person) comes from *privus*, meaning "single, individual." The opposite would be "public," meaning "of the people" (like Publicola).

People

Metellus Scipio (#2): Pompey's father-in-law, the father of Cornelia, and his co-consul for part of 52 B.C. Later he became the governor of Syria, and Pompey's lieutenant against Caesar. He was the adopted son of **Metellus Pius (#1)**, which is why their names are so similar.

Cornelia: Cornelia Metella, the fifth (and last) wife of Pompey

Appius: Appius Claudius Pulcher, a Roman general; the head of a powerful family; brother of **Clodius**; consul for 54 B.C. along with Lucius Domitius Ahenobarbus (#2). (His election was likely aided by the fact that his daughter had recently married Pompey's son)

Historic Occasions

52 B.C.: Pompey married **Cornelia Metella** (fifth wife), at the age of 54

50 B.C.: Paullus was consul, along with Marcellus Minor (#1). His cousin Marcellus Maior (#2) was elected consul for the next year, 49 B.C. The nicknames were given to keep them straight.

50 B.C.: Pompey's illness

On the Map

Naples: a city in southern Italy with a large harbour

Reading

Part One

Now Pompey returning into the city, married Cornelia, the daughter of **Metellus Scipio (#2)**; not a **maiden**, but late the widow of Publius Crassus the son, that was slain in Parthia. This lady had excellent gifts to be beloved besides her beauty. For she was properly learned, could play well on the harp, was skillful in music and geometry, and took great pleasure also in philosophy, and not vainly without some profit. For she was very modest and sober of behaviour, without brawling and foolish curiosity, which commonly young women have, that are endowed with such singular gifts. Her father also, was a nobleman, both in blood, and life.

Notwithstanding, these unlike marriages did not please some: for Cornelia was young enough to have been his son's wife. Now the best citizens thought that therein he regarded not the care of the commonwealth, being in such a troublesome time, which had chosen him only as **the remedy to redress the same**; and that he in the meantime gave himself over to marrying and feasting, where rather he should have been careful of his consulship, which was **disposed upon him against the law, for common calamity's sake,** that otherwise he had not have come by, if all had been quiet. Furthermore, he sharply proceeded against them which by bribery and unlawful means came to office: and having made laws and ordinances for the administration of justice otherwise, he dealt justly and uprightly in all things, giving safety, order, silence and gravity to matters of judgement, with force of arms, himself being present: saving that when his father-in-law was also accused among others, he sent for the three hundred and sixty judges home to his house, praying them to help him. Whereupon, when the accuser saw Scipio accompanied by the judges themselves, returning into the Forum, he **let fall his suit**.

[omission for length]

This inconstancy was much reproved in Pompey. Howbeit, otherwise he set all things in good order; and chose his father-in-law Scipio (#2) for his colleague and fellow in the consulship, for the five last months.

[Cato, as he had agreed, gave Pompey political advice (but in private). Among his concerns was that Caesar, understanding the power of money to buy more power, was building up support for himself. Cato was disappointed by Pompey's lack of action, so he ran for consul himself in the next election, but was not successful.]

Part Two

After that, Pompey caused the government of his provinces to be appointed to himself for four years more, with commission to take yearly out of the treasury a thousand talents to defray the charges of this war. Caesar's friends, seeing that Pompey was being so rewarded, prayed that there might also be had some consideration of him (Caesar) that had likewise won great wars for the empire of Rome; saying that his good service deserved either that they should make him consul again, or else that they should prolong his charge and government, so as he might yet peaceably enjoy the honour to command that which he had conquered, to the end that no other successor might reap the fruit of his labour.

There arising some debate about this, Pompey took it upon himself, as it were out of kindness to Caesar, to plead his cause and allay any jealousy that was conceived against him; telling them that he had letters from Caesar, expressing his desire for a successor, and his own discharge from the command; but it would be only right that they should give him leave to stand for the consulship though in his absence. Which Cato stoutly withstood, saying that Caesar must return home as a **private man**, and, leaving his army, should come in person to **crave recompense** of his country. But because Pompey made no reply nor answer to the contrary, men suspected straight that he had no great good liking of Caesar; and the rather, because he had sent unto him for the two legions which he had lent him, under colour of his war against the Parthians. However, Caesar, though he well knew why they were asked for, sent them home very liberally rewarded.

Part Three

About that time, Pompey fell sick at **Naples** of a dangerous disease, whereof, notwithstanding, he recovered again. The Neapolitans thereupon, by persuasion of Praxagoras, one of the chiefest men of their city, did sacrifice to the gods for his recovery. The like did also their neighbours round about: and in fine, it ran so generally through all Italy, that there was no city or town (great or small) but made open feast and rejoicing for many days together. Besides, the infinite number of people was such, that went to meet him out of all parts, that there was not place enough for them all; but the highways, cities, towns and ports of the sea were all full of people, feasting and sacrificing to the gods, and rejoicing for his recovery. Divers also went to meet him, crowned with garlands, and so did attend on him, casting **nosegays** and flowers upon him.

Thus was his journey the noblest sight that ever was, all the way as he came: howbeit men thought also, that this was the chiefest cause of the beginning of the civil wars. For he fell into such a pride, and glorious conceit of himself, with the exceeding joy he took to see himself thus honoured: that forgetting his orderly government, which made all his former doings to prosper, he grew too bold in despising of Caesar's power, as though he stood in no need of other power or care to withstand him, but that he could overcome him as he would, far more easily than he could have done before.

Besides this, **Appius**, under whose command those legions which Pompey lent to Caesar were returned, coming lately out of Gaul, spoke slightingly of Caesar's actions there, and spread scandalous reports about him. For he said that Pompey knew not his own strength and authority, that would seek to make himself strong, by other power against him: considering that he (Pompey) might overcome him (Caesar) with his own legions he should bring with him, so soon as they saw but Pompey in the face, such ill-will did Caesar's own soldiers bear him, and were marvellous desirous besides to see himself.

These flattering tales so puffed up Pompey, and brought him into such a security and trust of himself, that he mocked them to scorn which were afraid of wars. And to those also which said, that if Caesar came to Rome, they saw not how they could resist his power: he smilingly answered them again, and bade them take no thought for that: "For as oft," said he, "as I do but stamp my foot upon the ground of Italy, I shall bring men enough out of every corner, both footmen and horsemen."

Narration and Discussion

Why was Pompey's new marriage criticized, even though Cornelia was an admirable individual (and perhaps a good influence)?

Do you think Pompey had changed his mind about the morality of bribes and similar means of persuasion?

Plutarch says that the extreme love and praise shown to Pompey gave him "pride and a glorious conceit of himself." How did that influence his decision to fight against Caesar?

Creative narration: This would be a good lesson in which to do a "Pompey Podcast" or some on-the-street interviewing.

Lesson 19

Introduction

In 50 B.C., the big debate in the Roman Senate was how serious a problem it was to have two competing rulers, each with an army, and each army (technically) outside of Rome (so still legal). Would it work for Pompey and Caesar each to have a small army (say one legion), and to promise to "play nice?" Or was complete dismissal of all troops the only answer? The events of early 49 B.C. made it clear that such arguments were a waste of time: a civil war had already begun.

Vocabulary

nearer unto Italy: that is, from Gaul

won with money: bribed, bought off

tended to this end: seemed to be going in the same direction

read a letter unto the people: see note under **Mark Antony**

to be provided: to gather what they needed (such as weapons)

ambassadors: those sent to negotiate or capitulate (rather than fight)

Cato immediately departed into Sicily: The *Life of Cato* says that he went there to secure food supplies for Pompey's army.

Word Trivia

garboil: confusion and disturbance. It comes from French, Italian, and Latin words that meant to boil and seethe.

People

Paullus: Lucius Aemilius Lepidus Paullus; son of **Lepidus (#1)**; brother to **Lepidus #2**; consul for 50 B.C. with **Marcellus Minor (#1)** (see note in previous lesson)

Curio: Gaius Scribonius Curio Burbulieus, a statesman and orator, elected tribune of the people for 50 B.C. He began to support Julius Caesar at that time, apparently because Caesar paid off his debts. At the end of his year as tribune, he travelled to meet with Caesar, and brought back the document which was read soon after in the Senate. After fleeing Rome (see **Mark Antony**), he became a commander in Caesar's army, and died in battle later that same year.

Mark Antony or **Antony:** Marcus Antonius, Roman general, supporter of Caesar; later part of the Second Triumvirate. He also took over the position of tribune which **Curio** had held in the previous year, and began on January 1st by reading the document with Caesar's demands. However, this did not go as well as hoped, and he, along with Curio and others, fled from Rome to join Caesar's camp.

Marcellus Maior (#2): cousin to **Marcellus Minor (#1)**; consul for 49 B.C. He took office on January 1 along with **Lentulus Crus** (not to be confused with **Lepidus**) and was immediately notified that Julius Caesar was declaring war on Rome.

Tullus: Lucius Volcatius Tullus, a Roman politician who had been consul in 66 B.C.

Phaonius: or Favonius

Historic Occasions

January 10, 49 B.C.: Julius Caesar crossed the **Rubicon River** with his army, an act of defiance which was also a declaration of war

On the Map

Rubicon River: the boundary between Cisalpine Gaul and Italy. (The Rubicon in present-day Italy is believed to be the same river.)

Reading

Part One

In the meantime, Caesar gathered force still unto him, and thenceforth drew **nearer unto Italy**. He sent of his soldiers daily to Rome to be present at the election of the magistrates, and many of them that were in office, he **won with money**: amongst whom was **Paullus**, one of the consuls, whom he won of his side by means of a thousand five hundred talents; and **Curio**, the tribune of the people, whom he discharged of an infinite debt he owed; together with **Mark Antony**, who, out of friendship to Curio, had become bound with him in the same obligations for them all. Furthermore, it was found that a captain or centurion sent from Caesar, being near unto the Senate, understanding that the council would not prolong Caesar's government which he required, clapping his hand upon the handle of his sword: "Well," said he, "this shall give it him."

So, to be short, all that was done and said **tended to this end**.

Notwithstanding, the petitions and requests that Curio made on Caesar's behalf seemed somewhat more reasonable for the people: for he requested one of two things: either to make Pompey to put down his army, or else to permit Caesar to have his army as well as he. For, either being both made private men, they would fall to agreement of themselves: or else being both of like strength, neither of both would seek any alteration, fearing one another, but would content themselves either of them with their own. Or otherwise, he that should weaken the one and strengthen the other should double his power whom he feared. Thereto very hotly replied the consul **Marcellus (probably #1)**, calling Caesar a thief; and said that he should be proclaimed an open enemy to Rome if he did not disperse his army.

This notwithstanding, in fine **Curio**, with the assistance of **Antony** and Piso, procured that the Senate should decide the matter. "For," said he, "all those that would have Caesar leave his army, and Pompey to keep his, let them stand on the one side." Thereupon the most part of them stood at one side. Then he bade them again come away from them, that would have them both leave their armies. Then there remained only but two and twenty that stood for Pompey: and all the rest went to Curio's side. Then Curio, looking aloft for joy at the victory, went into the Forum, and there was received of his tribune faction with shouts of joy and clapping of hands, and infinite nosegays and garlands of flowers thrown upon him.

Pompey was not then present to see the Senators' good will towards him: because by the law, such as have commandment over soldiers cannot enter into Rome. Notwithstanding, Marcellus, standing up, said that he would not stand trifling hearing of orations and arguments, when he knew that ten legions were already passed over the Alps, intending to come in arms against them; and that he would send a man unto them that should defend their country well enough.

Upon this the city went into mourning, as in a public calamity, and Marcellus, accompanied by the Senate, went solemnly through the Forum to meet Pompey, and made him this address: "Pompey, I command thee to help thy country with that army thou hast already, and also to levy more to aid thee."

[omission for length]

Part Two

Now when Pompey thought to levy soldiers in Rome, some would not obey him; a few others went unwillingly to him with heavy hearts; and the most of them cried, "Peace, peace." Antony also, against the Senate's mind, **read a letter unto the people**, sent from Caesar and containing certain offers and reasonable requests, and Antony did this to draw the common people's affection towards him (Caesar). For Caesar's request was that Pompey and he should, both of them, resign their governments, and should dismiss their armies to make all well, referring themselves wholly to the judgement of the people, and to deliver up account unto them of their doings.

Lentulus, being now entered into his consulship for 49 B.C., along with **Marcellus #2**, did not assemble the Senate. But Cicero, lately returned out of Cilicia, tried to bring them to agreement, proposing that Caesar should leave Gaul, and all the rest of his army; reserving only two legions together with the government of Illyria; and should thus be put in nomination for a second consulship. Pompey liked not this motion, but Caesar's friends were contented to grant that he should have but one of his legions. But Lentulus still opposed it, and Cato cried out on the other side also, that Pompey did ill to be deceived again. So all treaty of peace was cut off.

Part Three

In the meantime, news came to Rome that Caesar had won Ariminum, a fair great city of Italy, and that he came directly to Rome with a great power. But that was not true. For he came but with three hundred horse soldiers, and five thousand footmen, and would not tarry for the rest of his army that was yet on the other side of the mountains in Gaul, but made haste rather to surprise his enemies upon the sudden, with them being afraid and in **garboil**, not looking for him so soon; rather than to give them time **to be provided**, and to fight with him when they were ready.

[omission for length: Caesar's crossing of the Rubicon, which has been described elsewhere]

Now the news of Caesar's coming being carried to Rome, they were in such a marvellous fear as the like was never seen. For all the Senate ran immediately unto Pompey, and all the other magistrates of the city fled unto him also. **Tullus**, asking Pompey what power he had to resist them: he answered him, faltering somewhat in his speech, that he had the two legions ready which Caesar sent back; and that he thought with the number of them which he had levied in haste, he should make up the number of thirty thousand fighting men. Then Tullus cried out openly: "Ah, thou hast mocked us, Pompey"; and thereupon gave order they should send **ambassadors** unto Caesar. There was one **Phaonius** in the company, who bade Pompey then stamp his foot upon the ground and make those soldiers come which he had promised them.

Pompey gently bore with Phaonius' mock. But when Cato told him also what he had prophesied beforehand of Caesar, he answered him again: "Indeed thou hast prophesied more truly than I, but I have dealt more friendly than he." Then Cato thought good that they should make Pompey lieutenant general of Rome with full and absolute power to command all, saying that the selfsame men which do the greatest mischief know best also how to remedy the same.

So **Cato immediately departed into Sicily**, having the charge and government of that country: and also every one of the other senators went unto the charge they were appointed.

Narration and Discussion

Did Caesar really intend to disband his army, or were his proposals only a deception, as Cato said?

What did Cato mean when he said that "the selfsame men which do the greatest mischief know best also how to remedy the same?"

Lesson 20

Introduction

"All the Senate ran immediately unto Pompey." Pompey's leadership was still sought in a crisis: so he would be the one to defend Rome against a threatened takeover by Julius Caesar.

Plutarch's chronology for this part of the story is a bit confusing, and he may have left out some details that he thought his readers would already know. These are the basic events: when Pompey and many of the senators fled from Rome (Part One), they did not intend to fight with Caesar (although they did have a sizeable army with them). Caesar went briefly to Rome; "possessed the city" (partly so that he could help himself to the funds to pay his soldiers); and then did pursue Pompey, but changed his tactics and went to Spain to capture Pompey's lieutenants (Part Two).

Knowing the real battles were still ahead, Pompey put his men into a program of intensive military and physical training (Part Three).

Vocabulary

credit: believe

Caesar's friends: that is, traitors

excepting only two vessels: Caesar did capture those two ships

liburnian: a type of small galley

sack: destroy and rob

part: side, position; used in the sense of "take someone's part"

Historic Occasions

49-45 B.C.: The Great Roman Civil War, also called Caesar's Civil War

49 B.C.: Caesar appointed Dictator, but resigned after eleven days

On the Map

Brundisium: see **Lesson Nine**. This was the main port for crossing into Greece, where Pompey planned to collect his forces and prepare for war. He apparently did not expect Caesar to follow them so quickly; and Caesar seems to have been hesitant to attack Brundisium, as it is said that he first sent Pompey's friend **Numerius** to negotiate peace terms. When Pompey refused, he did attack the city, and Pompey was forced to escape by sea (along with Numerius).

Dyrrhachium (sometimes Dyrrachium): a city located in what is now Albania. Pompey used Dyrrhachium as a storage site for supplies such as food; so Caesar hoped that if Pompey could be drawn away to fight elsewhere, his army might be cut off from those supplies.

Beroea: a town in Macedonia

Reading

Part One

Thus all Italy being in arms, no man knew what was best to be done.

For they that were outside of Rome came flying thither from all parts; and those, on the other side, that were within Rome, went out as fast, and forsook the city in this trouble and disorder. Those which might serve, being willing to obey, were found very weak; and those, on the other side, which by disobedience did hurt, were too strong and ill to be governed by the magistrates, having law to command. For there was no possibility to pacify their fear; neither would they suffer Pompey to offer things as he would; but every man followed his own fancy, even as he found himself grieved, afraid, or in doubt; so that even in the same day quite contrary counsels were acted upon. Pompey could hear nothing of certainty of his enemies. For someone would bring him news one way, and then someone else again another way: and then if he would not **credit** them, they were angry with him.

At the length, when he saw the tumult and confusion so great at Rome as there was no means to pacify it, he commanded all the senators to follow him; telling all them that remained behind that he would take them for **Caesar's friends**; and so at night departed out of the city. Then the two consuls fled also, without doing any sacrifice to the gods, as they were wont to do before they went to make any wars.

So Pompey, even in his greatest trouble and most danger, might think himself happy to have every man's goodwill as he had. For, though divers misliked the cause of this war, yet no man hated the captain: but there were more found that could not forsake Pompey for the love they bare him, than there were that followed him to fight for their liberty.

Part Two

Shortly after Pompey was gone out of Rome, Caesar was come to Rome: who, possessing the city, spoke very gently unto all them he found there, and pacified their fear; saving that he threatened Metellus (#3), one of the tribunes of the people, to put him to death, because he (Metellus) would not suffer him (Caesar) to take any of the treasure of the commonwealth. Unto that cruel threat he added a more bitter speech also, saying that it was not so hard a thing for him to do it, as to speak it. By this means removing Metellus, and taking what moneys were of use for his occasions, he set forward in pursuit of Pompey, endeavouring with all speed to drive him out of Italy before his army, that was in Spain, could join him.

But Pompey arriving at **Brundisium**, and having gotten some ships together, he made the two consuls presently embark with thirty ensigns of footmen, which he sent beyond the sea before unto **Dyrrhachium**. And immediately after that, he sent his father-in-law Scipio (#2) and his son Gnaeus Pompey into Syria, to provide him ships. Himself, on the other side, fortified the ramparts of the city, and placed the lightest soldiers he had upon the walls, and commanded the Brundisians not to stir out of their houses; and further, he cast trenches within the city, at the end of the streets in divers places, and filled those trenches with sharp pointed stakes, saving two streets only, which went unto the harbour. Then the third day after, having embarked all the rest of his soldiers at his pleasure, he suddenly lifting up a sign into the air, to give them warning which he had left to guard the ramparts: they straight ran to him with speed, and quickly receiving them into his ships, he weighed anchor, and hoisted sail.

Caesar meantime perceiving their departure by seeing the walls unguarded, hastened after, and in the heat of pursuit was all but entangled himself among the stakes and trenches. But the Brundisians discovering the danger to him, and showing him the way, he wheeled about, and taking a circuit round the city, made towards the haven, where he found all the ships on their way **excepting only two vessels** that had but a few soldiers aboard. Some think that this departure of Pompey was one of the best stratagems of war that ever he used. Notwithstanding, Caesar marvelled much that Pompey, being in a strong city, and looking for his army to come out of Spain, and being master of the sea besides, would ever forsake Italy. However, it appeared plainly, and Caesar showed it by his actions, that he was in great fear of delay; for when he had taken **Numerius** (a friend of Pompey's) prisoner, he sent him as an ambassador to Brundisium, with offers of peace and reconciliation upon equal terms; but Numerius sailed away with Pompey.

Part Three

And now Caesar having become master of all Italy in sixty days, without a drop of blood shed, had a great desire forthwith to follow Pompey. But because he had no ships ready, he let him go, and hasted towards Spain, to join Pompey's army there unto his.

Now Pompey in the mean space, had gotten a marvellous great power together both by sea and by land. His army by sea was wonderful. For he had five hundred good ships of war, and of light vessels, **liburnians**, and others, an infinite number. By land, he had all the flower of the horsemen of Rome, and of all Italy, to the number of seven thousand horse, all rich men, of great houses, and valiant minds. But his footmen, they were men of all sorts, and raw soldiers untrained, whom Pompey continually exercised, lying at the city of **Beroea**, not sitting idly, but performing exercises as if he had been in the prime of his youth. Which was to great purpose to encourage others, seeing Pompey, being eight and fifty years old, able to fight afoot, armed at all pieces; and then a-horseback, quickly to draw out his sword while his horse was in his full career, and easily to put it up again; and to throw his dart from him, not only with such agility to hit point blank, but also with strength to cast it such a way from him, that few young men could do the like.

[omission for length: some military details]

Pompey's officers sat in council, and following Cato's opinion, decreed that they should put no citizen of Rome to death but in battle; and that they should **sack** no city that was subject to the empire of Rome: the which made Pompey's **part** the better liked. For they that had nothing to do with the wars, either because they dwelt far off, or else for that they were so poor, as otherwise they were not regarded: did yet both in deed and word favour Pompey's part, thinking anyone an enemy both to the gods and men that wished not Pompey victory.

Narration and Discussion

In Part One, why did Pompey and the senators leave Rome? Should they not have stayed to defend it?

Describe Pompey's training camp at Beroea.

For older students: Plutarch suggests that Pompey's soldiers followed him more out of loyalty than they did out of concern for their liberty. Did their motivation really matter?

Lesson 21

Introduction

In July of 48 B.C. the two armies fought the Battle of Dyrrhachium, and Caesar's army barely missed being destroyed by Pompey's forces. Pompey then followed Caesar into Thessaly, hoping to besiege him or exhaust his resources; but the stage was already set for their final battle.

Vocabulary

Pompey's army that was in Spain: Caesar's march to Spain and his capture of Pompey's troops is detailed in other histories. With this additional military power, he then returned to Italy, crossed the Adriatic Sea, and quickly took the port of **Oricum.**

commodious: large enough

Once only: that is, at the Battle of Dyrrhachium

This victory: This was a victory for Pompey's side, in spite of Caesar's remark that they lacked a "victor." However, Pompey realized he was not really in a position to continue to fight against Caesar.

they would needs hazard battle: they were in the mood to fight

bickering: skirmish, bit of fighting

bridle: restrain

marched forward to follow Caesar: see **On the Map**, below

determined not to give him battle: see **Discussion Questions**

straight: immediately

imputations: insinuations, hints

Time Trivia

Julius Caesar held the special position of Pontifex Maximus in Rome, which included the responsibility for adjusting the calendar at the end of each year, since the Roman calendar did not line up properly with the rotation of the Earth around the sun. However, Caesar had been so busy with other things that he had forgotten to change the calendar. His arrival at **Oricum** took Bibulus by surprise, because Bibulus thought it was already winter, and he didn't expect anyone to risk the crossing. Caesar's absent-mindedness unexpectedly paid off.

People

Marcus Calpurnius Bibulus: (102 B.C.-48 B.C.), the same **Bibulus** who had been consul with Caesar. He was assigned to keep Caesar's forces from crossing from Italy, but was surprised by their untimely arrival at **Oricum** (see **Time Trivia**, above), and failed to stop their occupation of the port. He died soon afterwards. (More trivia: **Bibulus** was the first husband of Porcia (or Portia) who later married **Brutus (#3)**.)

Labienus, general of the horsemen: Titus Labienus, who had been a lieutenant under Caesar but who now opposed him

Phaonius: see **Lesson 20**

Gnaeus Domitius Calvinus, or **Domitius Calvinus (Domitius #3): Roman general, senator, and consul; lieutenant in Caesar's army.**

Metellus Scipio (#2): see **Lesson 18.**

Historic Occasions

48 B.C.: Caesar captured Oricum

48 B.C.: Caesar reappointed Dictator

July, 48 B.C.: Battle of Dyrrhachium

On the Map

Oricum: a port in **Epirus**, the region west of Macedonia

Dyrrhachium: see **Lesson 20**

Thessaly: a region of Greece

Reading

Part One

Caesar also showed himself very merciful and courteous, where he overcame. For when he had won all **Pompey's army that was in Spain**, he allowed the captains that were taken to go at liberty, and only reserved the soldiers. Then coming over the Alps again, he passed through all Italy, and came to the city of Brundisium in the winter quarter; and there passing over the sea, he went unto the city of **Oricum**, and landed there. And having Jubius, an intimate friend of Pompey's, with him as his prisoner, he dispatched him to Pompey with an invitation that they, meeting together in a conference, should disband their armies within three days, and renewing their former friendship with solemn oaths, should return together into Italy.

Pompey looked upon this again as some new stratagem, and therefore marching down in all haste to the seacoast, possessed himself of all forts and places of strength suitable to encamp in; and to secure his land-forces, as likewise of all ports and harbours commodious to receive any that came by sea: so that what wind soever blew on the sky, it served his turn, to bring him either men, victuals, or money. Caesar, on the other side, was so hemmed in both by sea and land that he was forced to desire battle, daily provoking the enemy, and assailing them in their very forts; and in these light skirmishes for the most part had the better.

[Both sides suffered shortages of food, but it appeared that Caesar's side would soon have the advantage of the coming grain harvest. Pompey needed to act quickly.]

Part Two

Once only Caesar was dangerously overthrown, and was within a little of losing his whole army, Pompey having fought nobly, routing the whole force and killing two thousand on the spot. But either he was not able, or was afraid, to go on and force his way into their camp with them; so that Caesar made the remark that "Today the victory had been the enemy's, had there been anyone among them to gain it."

This victory at Dyrrhachium put Pompey's men in such courage, that **they would needs hazard battle**. And Pompey himself also, though he wrote letters unto strange kings, captains, and cities of his confederacy, as if he had already won all: he was yet afraid to fight another battle, choosing rather by delays and distress of provisions to tire out a body of men who had never yet been conquered by force of arms, and who had long been used to fight and conquer together; while their time of life, now an advanced one, which made them quickly weary of those other hardships of war, such as were long marches and frequent decamping, making trenches, and building fortifications, made them eager to come to close combat and venture a battle with all speed.

But notwithstanding that Pompey had before persuaded his men to be quiet, and not to stir (perceiving that, after this last **bickering**, Caesar, being short of victuals, raised his camp, and departed thence to go into **Thessaly**, through the country of the Athamanians). Then Pompey could no more **bridle** the glory and courage of those who cried, "Caesar is fled, let us follow him." But others said, "Let us return home again into Italy."

[omission]

Part Three

Thereupon, assembling Pompey's war council, Afranius thought it best to win Italy, for that was the chiefest mark to be shot at in this war: for whosoever obtained that, had straight all Sicily, Sardinia, Corsica, Spain, and Gaul at commandment. Furthermore, that it was a dishonour to Pompey (which in reason should touch him above all things) to suffer their own country to be in such cruel bondage and subjection unto slaves and flatterers of tyrants, offering itself as it were into their hands.

But Pompey neither thought it honourable for him once again to flee from Caesar, and to make him follow him, since Fortune had given him opportunity to have Caesar in chase; nor lawful also, before the gods, to forsake his father-in-law Scipio (#2), and many others also that had been consuls, dispersed abroad in Greece and Thessaly; which should immediately fall into Caesar's hands, with all their riches and armies they had. Furthermore, he said, that they had care enough for the city of Rome, which drew the wars farthest off from them: so as, they remaining safe and quiet at home, (neither hearing nor feeling the misery of wars) might, in the end, peaceably receive and welcome him home that remained conqueror.

Interlude

What did Caesar do after the Battle of Dyrrhachium? Pompey chased Caesar for about four days, while Caesar took care of necessary tasks such as getting care for wounded men and paying his soldiers. He was also trying to get to his lieutenant Domitius (#3) before Pompey did. Caesar continued to have food supply problems which were caused partly because most of the local inhabitants supported Pompey; and Pompey, knowing this, was hopeful that Caesar would surrender out of frustration. However, all this changed with the arrival of Mark Antony's troops from Italy.

Part Four

With this determination, he **marched forward to follow Caesar**, being **determined not to give him battle**, but to besiege him, and only to compass him in still being near unto him, and so to cut him off from victuals. There was also another reason that made him to follow that determination. For it was reported to him, that there was a speech given out among the Roman knights, that so soon as ever they had overcome Caesar, they must also bring Pompey to be a private man again. Some say therefore, that Pompey would never afterwards employ Cato in any greater matters of weight in all this war, but when he followed Caesar, he left him captain of his army to keep his carriage by sea, fearing that so soon as Caesar were once overcome, Cato would make him **straight** also resign his authority.

While he was thus slowly attending the motions of the enemy, he was exposed on all sides to outcries and **imputations** of using his own generalship to defeat, not Caesar, but his country and the Senate, that he might always continue in authority, and never cease to keep those for his guards and servants who themselves claimed to govern the world.

[The following section contains several omissions for length.]

The persuasions and mocking speech of others compelled Pompey in the end (who could not abide to be ill spoken of, and would not deny his friends anything) to follow their vain hope and desires, and to forsake his own wise determination: the which thing, no good shipmaster, and much less a chief and sovereign captain, over so many nations and so great armies, should have suffered, and consented unto.

All this notwithstanding, they of Pompey's side still being importunate of him, and troubling him in this sort: in fine, when they were come into the fields of Pharsalus, they compelled Pompey to call a council. There **Labienus, general of the horsemen**, standing up, swore before them all that he would not return from the battle, before he had made his enemies to flee. The like oath all the rest did take.

Narration and Discussion

Pompey hoped to avoid outright battle with Caesar by, perhaps, besieging him somewhere and forcing him to surrender. He at first refused to allow his troops to be drawn into battle; for instance, by placing them on uneven ground where he knew it would be difficult to engage. However, the arguments of others finally convinced him to fight. Was this the right choice? (Did he have any other?)

Lesson 22

Introduction

At the short Battle of Pharsalus in August, Caesar was the unquestioned winner. Pompey, stunned by this defeat, escaped, as they say, "with his life."

Vocabulary

raise his camp: Caesar had planned to break camp and go to Scotussa, until he heard that Pompey's troops were preparing to fight.

voward: those troops in the front

straitly: strictly

six cohorts…: about 3,000 fighting men, counting 500 in a cohort

mistrusting: suspecting

People

Gaius Crassinius: captain in Caesar's army

Historic Occasions

August, 48 B.C.: Battle of Pharsalus

On the Map

Pharsalus: the exact location of the battle appears to be uncertain. Caesar called it "the battle in **Thessalia**," so for our purposes, locating that region should be enough.

Reading

Part One

At the break of the day, Caesar determined to **raise his camp**, and to go to Scotussa, a city in Thessaly. As his soldiers were busy about overthrowing of their tents, and sending away their bags and baggage, there came scouts unto him that brought him word they saw a great deal of armour and weapons carried to and fro in their enemies' camp; and heard a noise and bustling besides, as of men that were preparing to fight. After these came in other scouts, that brought word also that Pompey's **voward** was already set in battle array. Then Caesar said that the day was now come they had longed for so sore; and that they should now fight with men, not with hunger: and he instantly gave orders for the red colours to be set up before his tent, which was the sign all the Romans used to show that they would fight. The soldiers, seeing that, left their carriage and tents; and with great shouts of joy ran to arm themselves. The captains of every band, also, bestowed every man in such place as he should fight; and so they conveyed themselves into battle array, without any tumult or disorder, as quietly as if they should have entered into a dance.

Pompey himself led the right wing of his army against Antony. The middle of the battle he gave unto Scipio his father-in-law, being right against Domitius Calvinus (#3). The left wing also was led by Lucius Domitius Ahenobarbus (#2), the which was guarded with men of arms. For all the horsemen were placed on that side, to distress Caesar if they could, that was directly against them; and to overthrow the Tenth Legion that was so much accounted of, being the most valiant soldiers the enemy had in all his army, amongst the which Caesar did ever use to fight in person.

Pompey being a-horseback, rode up and down to consider the ordinance of both battles: and perceiving that his enemies stood still in their ranks, looking for the signal of battle, and that his own battle array on the other side waved up and down disorderly, as men unskillful in wars: he was afraid they would flee before they were charged. Thereupon he **straitly** commanded those at the front that they should steadily keep their ranks, and standing close together should so defend themselves, receiving the charge of the enemy.

In Caesar's army, there were about two and twenty thousand fighting men; and in Pompey's army, somewhat above twice as many. Most men, of course, were fully occupied with their own matters; only some few of the noblest Romans, together with certain Greeks there present, standing as spectators, without the battle, seeing the armies now ready to join, began to bethink them to what pass the ambition and willful contention between these two men had brought the state of Rome. For the weapons of kinsmen, the bands of brethren, the ensigns all alike, the flower of so many valiant men of one city, did serve for a notable example to shew how man's nature pricked forward with covetousness, is quite blind and without reason. For if they could have been contented quietly to have governed that which they had conquered: the greatest, and best part of the world, both by sea and by land, was subject unto them. Or otherwise, if they could not have quenched their insatiable desire of victory and triumph, they had occasion of war enough offered them against the Parthians and Germans. Furthermore, they had enough to do besides to conquer Scythia, and the Indians: and withal, they had had an honest colour to have cloaked their ambitious desires, if it had been but to have brought the barbarous people to a civil life. For what horsemen of Scythia, or arrows of Parthia, or riches of Indians, could have abidden the power of three score and ten thousand Roman soldiers, and specially being led by two so famous captains as Pompey and Caesar—whose names these strange and far nations understood, long before the name of the Romans: so great were their victories, having conquered so many wild and barbarous people. They both being then in arms the one against the other, not regarding their honour, which made them so ambitious: did not spare their own country, who had until that time remained invincible, both in fame and prowess. For the alliance that was made between them, the love of Julia, and marrying with her, was suspected from the beginning to be but a deceit, and a pledge as it were of a conspiracy made between them, for a private benefit, more than for any true friendship.

Part Two

Now, when the fields of Pharsalus were covered over with men, with horses and armour; and the signal of battle was given on either side: the first man of Caesar's army that advanced forward to give charge was **Gaius Crassinius**, captain of six score and five men, to perform a great promise which he had made unto Caesar. For Caesar, when he came out of his tent in the morning, seeing him, called him to him by his name, and asked him what he thought of the success of this battle. Crassinius holding out his right hand unto him, courageously cried: "Oh Caesar, thine is the victory, and this day thou shalt commend me either alive or dead." Then remembering these words, he broke out of the ranks; and many following after him, he ran amongst the midst of his enemies. Straight they came to the sword, and made great slaughter. But he pressing forward still, one with a thrust ran him through the mouth, that the sword's point came through at his neck. Thereupon Crassinius being slain, the battle was equal.

Pompey did not make his left wing march over suddenly, but stayed, and cast his eyes abroad to see what his horsemen would do, the which had already divided their companies, meaning to compass in Caesar, and to make the small number of horsemen which he had before him to give back upon the squadron of his footmen. On the other side, as soon as Caesar had given the signal of battle, his horsemen retired back a little, and the **six cohorts which he had placed secretly behind them** (being three thousand fighting men) ran suddenly to assail the enemy upon the flank; and when they came near unto the horsemen, they threw the points of their darts upwards according to Caesar's commandment, and hit the young gentlemen full in their faces. They being utterly unskillful to fight, and least of all looking for such manner of fight, had not the hearts to defend themselves, nor to abide to be hurt as they were in their faces; but turning their heads, and clapping their hands on their faces, shamefully fled.

Caesar's men, however, did not follow them, but marched upon the foot, and attacked the wing, which the flight of the cavalry had left unprotected, and liable to be turned and taken in the ear; so that this wing now being attacked in the flank by these, and charged in the front by the Tenth Legion, was not able to abide the charge, or make any longer resistance, especially when they saw themselves surrounded and circumvented in the very way in which **they had designed to surround the enemy**. Thus these being likewise routed and put to flight, when Pompey, by the dust flying in the air, conjectured the fate of his horse, it were very hard to say what his thoughts or intentions were; but looking like one distracted and beside himself, and without any recollection or reflection that he was Pompey the Great, he retired slowly towards his camp, without speaking a word to any man, exactly according to the description in Homer's verses:

> But mighty Jove who sits aloft in ivory chariot high,
>
> Struck Ajax with so great a fear that Ajax by and by
>
> Let fall his leathern target made of tough ox hide sevenfold.
>
> And ran away, not looking back, for all he was so bold.

In this state Pompey entered into his tent, and sat him down there a great while; and spoke never a word: until such time as many of the enemies burst into the camp. And then, he said no more than, "What, even into our camp?" And so rising up, he put a gown on his back, even fit for his misfortune, and secretly stole out of the camp. The other legions also fled; and great slaughter was made of the tent-keepers, and their servants that guarded the camp.

[omission for length]

Part Three

When Pompey was gone a little way from his camp, he forsook his horse, having a very few with him: and perceiving that no man pursued him, he went afoot fair and softly, his head full of such thoughts and imaginations, as might be supposed a man of his like calling might have, who for four-and-thirty years' space together was wont continually to carry victory away; and began then even in his last cast, to prove what it was to flee, and to be overcome: and who thought then, with himself, how in one hour's space he had lost the honour and riches which he had gotten in so many battles; whereby he was not long before followed and obeyed of so many thousand men of war, of so many horsemen, and of such a great fleet of ships on the sea, and then to go as he did in such poor estate, and with so small a train, that his very enemies who sought him, knew him not.

Thus when he was passed the city of Larissa, and coming to the Valley of Tempe: there being thirsty, he fell down on his belly, and drank of the river. Then rising up again, he went his way thence, and came to the sea side, and took a fisher's cottage where he lay all night. The next morning by break of the day, he went into a little boat upon the river, and took the freemen with him that were about him: and as for the slaves, he sent them back again, and did counsel them boldly to go to Caesar, and not to be afraid. Thus, rowing up and down the shore side in this little boat, he spied a great ship of burden in the main sea, riding at anchor, which was ready to weigh anchor, and to sail away. The master of the ship was a Roman named Peticius, who, though he was not familiarly acquainted with Pompey, yet knew him by sight very well.

[omission for length]

Clapping his head for anger, he commanded his mariners to let down his boat, and gave him his hand, calling him Pompey by his name, **mistrusting** (seeing him in that estate) what misfortune had happened to him. Thereupon, not looking to be entreated, nor that he should tell him of his mishap, he received him into his ship, and all those he would have with him: and then hoisted sail.

[omission for length]

Narration and Discussion

Why does Plutarch call the Battle of Pharsalus needless and wasteful?

Plutarch compares Pompey's defeat and "running away" to that of Ajax (*The Iliad*, Book XI). Alfred J. Church, in the chapter "The Wounding of the Chiefs" of *The Iliad for Boys and Girls*, describes the scene this way:

> "Then Zeus put fear into the heart of the great Ajax himself. He would not fly, but he turned round, throwing his great shield over his shoulder, and moved towards the ships slowly, step by step. It was as when a donkey breaks into a field and eats the standing corn, and the children of the village beat him with sticks. Their arms are weak, and the sticks are broken on the beast's back, for he is slow in going, nor do they drive him out till he has eaten his fill."

Do you agree with this comparison?

Lesson 23

Introduction

After the Battle of Pharsalus, Julius Caesar returned to Rome and was given parades of triumph for his victories overseas (though his defeat of Pompey was underplayed).

Vocabulary

family: Dryden says "servants"

late: recent

clemency: see **Lesson Four**

his own near connection: Caesar had been his father-in-law

designed towards Euphrates: Pompey had considered seeking refuge in Parthia, which was associated with the Euphrates River

The residue of his train: his remaining supporters

People

Cratippus: Cratippus of Pergamon, a friend of **Cicero**

King Juba: Juba I of Numidia

King Ptolemy: the new king of Egypt, co-ruler with Cleopatra (although she had been deposed and was at war with her brother)

Arsaces: Arsaces of Pontus

On the Map

Mytilene: a city on the Greek island of **Lesbos**

Pamphylia: a region of what was called Asia Minor, between Lycia and Cilicia, in present-day Turkey.

Seleucia: a city on the Tigris River, in present-day Iraq

Reading

Part One

Pompey passing then by the city of Amphipolis, crossed over from thence into the isle of **Lesbos**, to go fetch his wife Cornelia and his son, who were then in the city of **Mytilene**. As soon as he arrived at the port in that island, he dispatched a messenger into the city, with news very different from Cornelia's expectation. For she, by all the former messages and letters sent to please her, had been put in hopes that the war was ended at Dyrrhachium, and that there was nothing more remaining for Pompey but the pursuit of Caesar.

This messenger now finding her in this hope, had not the heart so much as to salute her, but, letting her understand rather by his tears than words the great misfortune Pompey had, told her she must dispatch quickly, if she would see Pompey with one ship only, and none of his, but borrowed. The young lady, hearing this news, fell down in a swoon before him, and neither spoke nor stirred of long time; but after she was come to herself, remembering that it was no time to weep and lament, she went with speed through the city unto the seaside. There **Pompey**, meeting her, took her in his arms, and embraced her. But she, sinking under him, fell down, and said:

> "This woe is from my hard fortune, not thine, good husband; that I see thee now brought to one poor ship, who before thou married thy unfortunate Cornelia, were wont to sail these seas with five hundred ships. Alas, why art thou come to see me, and why didst thou not leave me to cursed fate and my wicked destiny: since myself am cause of all this thy evil? Alas, how happy a woman had I been, if I had been dead before I heard of the death of my first husband Publius Crassus, whom the wretched Parthians slew!"

It is reported that Cornelia spoke these words, and that Pompey also answered her in this manner:

> "Peradventure, Cornelia mine, thou hast known a better Fortune, which hath also deceived thee, because she hath continued longer with me than her manner is. But

> since we are born mortal, we must patiently bear these troubles, and prove Fortune again. Neither is it any less possible to recover our former state than it was to fall from that into this."

When Cornelia heard him say so, she sent back into the city for her baggage and **family**.

Part Two

The Mytilenians also came openly to salute Pompey, and prayed him to come into the city, and to refresh himself: but Pompey would not, and gave them counsel to obey the conqueror, and not to fear anything; for Caesar was a just man, and of a courteous nature. Then Pompey, turning unto **Cratippus** the philosopher**,** who came among the citizens also to see him, made his complaint unto him and reasoned a little with him about divine Providence. Cratippus courteously yielded unto him, putting him still in better hope, fearing lest he would have grown too hot and troublesome if he had opposed him.

[Plutarch imagines the conversation that might have taken place if Cratippus had been inclined to argue with Pompey.]

> For Pompey at the length might have asked him what providence of the gods there had been in his doings. And Cratippus might have answered him that, for the ill government of the commonwealth at Rome, it was of necessity that it should fall into the hands of a sovereign prince.
>
> Peradventure Cratippus might then have asked him, "How and whereby, Pompey, wouldst thou make us believe, if thou hadst overcome Caesar, that thou wouldst have used thy good fortune better than he?"

But we must leave the divine power to act as
we find it to do.

Part Three

Pompey having taken his wife and friends aboard, set sail, making no port, or touching anywhere, but when he was necessitated to take in provisions or fresh water. The first city he came unto was **Attalia** in the country of **Pamphylia**. Thither came to him certain galleys out of Cilicia, and many soldiers also, insomuch he had three score senators of Rome again in his company. Then, understanding that his army by sea was yet whole; and that Cato had gathered together a great number of his soldiers after the overthrow, whom he had transported with him into Africa: he lamented and complained unto his friends that they had compelled him to fight by land, and not suffered him to help himself with his other force (wherein he was the stronger): and that he kept not still near unto his army by sea, that if fortune failed him by land, he might yet presently have repaired to his power ready by sea, to have resisted his enemy. To confess a truth, Pompey committed not so great a fault in all this war, neither did Caesar put forth a better device, than to make his enemy fight far from his army by sea.

Thus, Pompey being driven to attempt somewhat according to his small ability, he sent ambassadors unto the cities. To others, he went himself in person also to require money, wherewith he manned and armed some ships. This notwithstanding, fearing the sudden approach of his enemy, lest he (Caesar) should prevent before he could put any reasonable force in readiness for to resist him: he bethought himself what place he might best retire unto for his most safety. When he had considered of it, he thought that there was never a province of the Romans that could save and defend them. And for other strange realms, he thought Parthia, above all others, was the best place to receive them into at that present time, having so small power as they had.

Others of his council were of mind to go into Africa, unto **King Juba**. But his friend Theophanes said he thought it a great folly to leave Egypt which was but three days sailing from thence, and **King Ptolemy** (being but lately come to man's estate, and bound unto Pompey for the **late** friendship and favour his father found of him);

and to go put himself into the hands of the Parthians, the vilest and unfaithfullest nation in the world; and not to make any trial of the **clemency** of a Roman, and **his own near connection**, to whom if he would but yield to be second he might be the first and chief over all the rest, to go and place himself at the mercy of **Arsaces**, which even Crassus had not submitted to while alive. Further, he thought it an ill part also for him to go carry his young wife, of the noble house of Scipio, amongst the barbarous people who might injure her.

This argument alone, they say, was persuasive enough to divert his course, that was **designed towards Euphrates**, if it were so indeed that any counsel of Pompey's, and not some superior power, made him take this other way. Being determined therefore to flee into Egypt, he departed out of Cyprus in a galley of **Seleucia** with his wife Cornelia. **The residue of his train** embarked also, some into galleys, and others into merchant ships of great burden, and so safely passed the sea without danger.

Narration and Discussion

Why was it a mistake for Pompey to try to fight far from the land?

Try to put the conversation between Cornelia and Pompey into your own words. How did Pompey try to reassure her that they could "weather the storm" together?

For older students: Discuss the imagined conversation between Pompey and Cratippus. How might Pompey have answered Cratippus' final question?

Lesson 24 and Examination Questions

Introduction

By seeking refuge in Egypt, Pompey signed his own death warrant.

Vocabulary

meanness: shabbiness

his galley should have no water to bring him in: the water was too shallow for Pompey's men to bring their galley near the shore

slaves enfranchised: freed men

nine and fifty years old: Using the dates we have, Pompey would have turned 58 on his birthday (either just before or just after his death).

their bellies full: to their satisfaction

good hap: good fortune

Historic Occasions

September, 48 B.C.: death of Pompey at the age of 58

46 B.C.: Caesar and **Lepidus (#2)** were consuls. Lepidus was a strong supporter of Julius Caesar. He was later part of the Second Triumvirate with Octavian (Caesar Augustus) and Mark Antony.

45 B.C.: Caesar was sole consul

44 B.C.: death of Julius Caesar at the age of 55

On the Map

Egypt, the Nile, etc.: Most students will have some knowledge of Egypt, but it is worthwhile looking again at a map, such as that on pages 84-85 of Constable's *Atlas of Ancient Rome.*

Pelusium: a city in the Nile Delta

at his country house near Alba: Pompey had also intended to bury Julia there, but the Roman people insisted on giving her a public funeral and placing her urn in the Campus Martius (Field of Mars).

Reading

Part One

[Pompey sent a request for refuge to King Ptolemy of Egypt, who was then in the city of ***Pelusium****. Ptolemy was still quite young and under the influence of his tutor and other advisors. The dilemma they faced was whether they should risk either being ruled by Pompey and angering Caesar; or letting Pompey escape and angering Caesar. After discussing the matter, the council decided that the practical solution was to send someone to kill him.]*

They, being determined of this among themselves, gave Achillas commission to do it. He taking with him Septimius (who had charge aforetime under Pompey) and Salvius, another centurion, also, with three or four soldiers besides, they made towards Pompey's galley. In the meantime, all the chiefest of those who accompanied Pompey in this voyage were come into his ship to learn the event of their embassy. But when they saw the manner of their reception, that in appearance it was neither princely nor honourable, nor indeed in any way answerable to the hopes of Theophanes, or their expectation (for there came but a few men in a fisher's boat to meet them), they began to suspect the **meanness** of their entertainment, and gave warning to Pompey that he should row back his galley, whilst he was out of their reach, and make for the sea.

In the meantime, the boat drew near, and Septimius rose, and saluted Pompey in the Roman tongue, by the name of *Imperator*, as much as "Sovereign Captain"; and Achillas also spoke to him in the Greek tongue, and bade him come into his boat; because that by the shoreside, there was a great deal of mud and sandbanks, so that **his galley should have no water to bring him in**. At the very same time, they saw, afar off, divers of the king's galleys, which were arming with all speed possible; and all the shore besides full of soldiers.

Thus, though Pompey and his company would have altered their minds, they could not have told how to have escaped: and furthermore, if they had shown that they mistrusted the Egyptians, then they would have given the murderer occasion to have executed his cruelty. So, taking his leave of his wife Cornelia (who lamented his death before it came), he commanded two centurions to go down before him into the

Egyptians' boat, and Philip one of his **slaves enfranchised**, with another slave called Scynes.

When Achillas reached out his hand to receive him into his boat, Pompey turned him to his wife and son, and said these verses of Sophocles unto them:

> He that once enters at a tyrant's door
>
> Becomes a slave, though he were free before.

These were the last words he spoke unto his people, when he left his own galley, and went into the Egyptians' boat.

Part Two

The land being a great way off from his galley, when he saw never a man in the boat speak friendly unto him: beholding Septimius, he said unto him: "Methinks, my friend, I should know thee, for that thou hast served with me heretofore." The other nodded with his head that it was true, but gave him no answer, nor shewed him any courtesy. Pompey seeing that no man spoke to him, took a little book he had in his hand, in the which he had written an oration that he meant to make unto King Ptolemy, and began to read it.

When they came near the shore, Cornelia with her servants and friends about her, stood up in her ship in great fear, to see what should become of Pompey. So, she hoped well, when she saw many of the king's people on the shore, coming towards Pompey at his landing, as it were to receive and honour him. But even as Pompey took Philip his hand to arise more easily, Septimus came first behind him and thrust him through with his sword. Next unto him also, Salvius and Achillas drew out their swords in like manner. Pompey then did no more but took up his gown with his hands, and hid his face, and manly abided the wounds they gave him, only sighing a little.

Thus, being **nine and fifty years old**, he ended his life the next day after the day of his birth.

Part Three

They that rode at anchor in their ships, when they saw him murdered, gave such a fearful cry that it was heard to the shore: then weighing up their anchors with speed, they hoisted sail, and departed their way, having wind at will that blew a lusty gale as soon as they had gotten the main sea. The Egyptians which prepared to row after them, when they saw they were past their reach, and impossible to be overtaken, they let them go. Then, having stricken off Pompey's head, they threw his body overboard, for a miserable spectacle to all those that were desirous to see him. Philip his enfranchised bondman remained ever by it, until such time as the Egyptians had seen it **their bellies full**.

Then having washed his body with salt water, and wrapped it up in an old shirt of his, because he had no other shift to lay it in. Then seeking up and down about the sands, at last he found some rotten plans of a little fisher-boat, not much, but yet enough to make up a funeral pile for a naked body, and that not quite entire. As he was busy gathering the broken pieces of this boat together, thither came unto him an old Roman, who in his youth had served under Pompey, and said unto him: "O friend, what art thou that preparest the funerals of Pompey the Great?" Philip answered, that he was a bondman of his, enfranchised. "Well," said he, "thou shalt not have all this honour alone, I pray thee yet let me accompany thee in so devout a deed, that I may not altogether repent me to have dwelt so long in a strange country, where I have abidden such misery and trouble: but that to recompense me withal, I may have this **good hap** with mine own hands to touch Pompey's body, and to help to bury the only and most famous captain of the Romans."

[omission for length]

Epilogue

Not long after, Caesar also came into Egypt, that was in great wars, where Pompey's head was presented unto him: but he turned his head aside, and would not see it, and abhorred him that brought it, as a detestable murderer. Then taking Pompey's ring, his ring wherewith he sealed his letters, whereupon was graven a lion holding a sword: he burst out a-weeping.

Achillas and Pothinus he put to death. King Ptolemy himself also, being overthrown in battle by the River Nile, vanished away, and was never heard of after.

The ashes of Pompey's body were afterwards brought unto his wife Cornelia, who buried them **at his country house near Alba**.

Narration and Discussion

Tell how Pompey faced his probable death with courage.

How did Philip show more loyalty and compassion than most of Pompey's friends?

Art History: "Pompey's Head," though a grisly topic, has inspired a few works of art over the years, and some students may be interested in researching this further. One example is *Caesar Contemplating the Head of Pompey*, by Giovanni (Giambattista) Tiepolo (1696-1770).

Creative narration: If you have been doing regular or occasional Pompey Podcasts, or even if you haven't, this would be a good time to gather material together for a "tribute" episode.

Examination Questions for Part Two

1. **Younger Students:** Tell a story to show how Pompey "fell into such a pride and glorious conceit of himself."

2. Describe how Pompey ran away, "not looking back for all he was so bold."

Older Students:

1. Describe the third triumph of Pompey. Why does Plutarch say, "O, happy would it have been for him if he had died when he had Alexander's fortune?"

2. (For high school students) "So great an empire…could not contain the covetous desire of these two men." Give some account of Pompey and Caesar in this connection.

Themistocles

(ca. 527-460/459 B.C.)

> "Themistocles said that indeed he could offer no skill to tune a harp, nor a viol, nor to play of a **psaltery**: but if they did put a city into his hands that was of small name, weak, and little, he knew ways enough how to make it noble, strong, and great."
>
> "Hereby it appeareth that he only of all others was at that time the original cause of the saving of Greece, and did most advance the honour and glory of the Athenians, by making them to overcome their enemies by force, and their friends and allies with liberality."

The World of Themistocles

The Persian Empire was formed in about 550 B.C. by Cyrus the Great, and at that time was ruled by the Achaemenid Dynasty. The Persians, commanding an unparalleled military force, thought Greece would be an easy addition to their map. To their surprise, the Greek city-states (although they often fought among themselves) were stubbornly courageous in the face of a common enemy.

Who was Themistocles?

Themistocles was an Athenian statesman and general during the Persian Wars. As a young man, Themistocles fought in the Battle of Marathon, which is briefly mentioned in this story. He would go on to lead the allied Greek forces at the major battles of Artemisium and Salamis.

His post-war attempts to rebuild the city of Athens were soured by political rivalry and, eventually, ostracism; and the damage was increased by accusations of treason which meant he could never return. Themistocles, though, usually had a "Plan B."

Personal Life

Themistocles' own family is not mentioned much in this story, but he was married at least once, to a woman named Archippe, and had several sons and daughters. Some biographers say that the family members were eventually able to join him in his exile in Persia.

Themistocles Trivia

As governor of Magnesia in his final years, Themistocles is believed to have been the first ruler ever to put his own portrait on coins.

For Extra Reading

The 1978 book *Children of the Fox*, by Jill Paton Walsh, would make an age-appropriate supplement for this term. It is currently scarce and/or expensive, but worth trying to locate through interlibrary loan. The book is divided into stories about three Greek children, connected only through the character of Themistokles (the spelling used in the book). The first story, about a girl named Aster, correlates with the lessons about the Battle of Salamis. The second, set in Sparta, fits into **Lesson Seven**; and the third, about King Admetus and Queen Phthia, into **Lesson Nine**.

Top Ten Terms in Themistocles

If you recognize these words, you're well on your way to mastering North's vocabulary. (They will not be noted in the lessons.)

1. **barbarian:** In this story, "barbarian" usually equals Persian. **Mede** is also used to mean Persian.
2. **Grecian, Greek:** In this *Life*, Grecian usually refers to "the other Greeks," those who were not of Athens. Dryden used the word "Greek," but North preferred "Grecian."
3. **haven:** harbour. Before Themistocles' time, the Athenians had used the port of **Phaleron**; but in 493 B.C. they began work on a new port and ship-building yard at the nearby town of **Piraeus**.
4. **isthmus:** A narrow strip of land (or "land bridge") joining two larger regions. The isthmus referred to here is the Isthmus of Corinth, which joins the northern and southern sections of Greece.
5. **Lacedaemonia:** another word for **Sparta**
6. **Olympic games:** a religious, cultural, and sporting event held every four years
7. ***Ostracismon*:** or Ostracism; a banishment, by the votes of the people, of those who threatened to become too powerful. This was quite new in Themistocles' time; it seems to have begun after the prosecution/persecution of Miltiades (see notes in **Lesson One**), as a means of preventing similar power struggles.
8. **practice, practise:** plan, plot, scheme. British/Canadian spelling differentiates between the noun and the verb; Americans use **practice** for both.
9. **strait:** tight, narrow. To be **strait** with people means to be restrictive (or stingy); to be "in a strait" means to be in a "tight spot," with few choices. A **strait** is also a narrow channel of water.
10. **strangers:** Many times in Plutarch, "strange" means "foreign" and "strangers" are often foreign mercenaries; but in this particular *Life*, "strangers" is used more often in the sense we know it, meaning unfamiliar people.

Lesson One

Introduction

When Themistocles was about fifteen years old, the government of Athens was suddenly overturned: the rule of tyrant kings gave way to democracy, and less control by wealthy families increased the power of common citizens. For Themistocles, this opened up career possibilities that would never have existed before, especially for someone with his temperament and skills in leadership. As soon as he was old enough, he ran for public office and was elected **Archon Eponymous**, the equivalent of "mayor." He soon had an introduction to warfare as well, at the **Battle of Marathon**.

Vocabulary

democratic, democracy: government in which a large amount of power is held by the citizens

alien or stranger: not from Athens

wrestling-place: a gymnasium. The Cynosarges was also a temple, and a place where lectures were given.

ingenious device: clever plot, strategy

vehement and impetuous: North says "hot-headed"

of a quick apprehension: intelligent, quick to learn

oration or declamation: a public speech. Themistocles memorized famous speeches, and created new ones of his own.

master: teacher

sagacity: wisdom

psaltery: a musical instrument played by plucking its strings

natural philosophy: science

Melissus was captain of the Samians against Pericles: See Plutarch's *Life of Pericles*. The point is that all this happened too late for Melissus to have been one of Themistocles' teachers.

a certain knowledge to handle great causes: we might say that he majored in political science and law

gave himself to state: became involved in public matters

even at his first entry: Themistocles was elected **Archon Eponymous** when he turned thirty.

at pike against: in conflict with or opposition to

bore the sway and government: Dryden says "the most powerful and influential leaders"

People

Stesimbrotus: a historian, one of Plutarch's sources

Anaxagoras: a philosopher in Athens, also mentioned in *Life of Pericles*

Melissus: a philosopher and a naval commander

Pericles: Athenian statesman, subject of Plutarch's *Life of Pericles*

Mnesiphilus: one of Themistocles' early teachers

Aristides: Athenian statesman, subject of Plutarch's *Life of Aristides*

Captain Miltiades: Athenian general, and the father of Themistocles' political rival **Cimon**

Historic Occasions

530 B.C.: Birth of Aristides

c. 524 B.C.: Birth of Themistocles

510-507 B.C.: Establishment of **democratic** government in Athens

c. 495 B.C.: Birth of **Pericles**

494 B.C.: Themistocles elected **Archon Eponymous** for the following year

490 B.C.: Battle of Marathon

489 B.C.: Death of Miltiades (A failed expedition after **Marathon** not only wounded him, but gave political rivals opportunity to attack his leadership. He was charged with "deceiving the Athenian people," and died soon afterwards.)

On the Map

As an introduction to this *Life*, it would be useful to look at maps of ancient Greece and the Persian Empire. Locate Athens, in the region of Attica; Sparta, in the Peloponnesus; and the Isthmus of Corinth. It would also be good to look for **Euboea** and **Boeotia**.

Phrearrhioi: a suburb of Athens belonging to the Leontis tribe. Its inhabitants were called **Phrearrhians**.

Reading

Part One

The birth of Themistocles was somewhat too obscure to do him honour. His father, Neocles, was of small reputation in Athens, being of **Phrearrhioi** and the tribe of Leontis; his mother was an **alien or stranger**.

[omission for length: speculation about the background of Themistocles' mother]

As "illegitimate" children, including those that were of half-blood or had but one parent an Athenian, had to attend at the Cynosarges (a **wrestling-place** outside the gates, dedicated to Hercules, who was also of half-blood amongst the gods, having had a mortal woman for his mother), Themistocles persuaded several of the young men of high birth to accompany him to anoint and exercise themselves together at

Cynosarges; an **ingenious device** for destroying the distinction between the noble and the base-born, and between those of the "whole" and those of the half-blood of Athens.

[brief omission]

It is confessed by all that from his youth he was of a **vehement and impetuous** nature, **of a quick apprehension**, and a strong and aspiring bent for action and great affairs. The holidays and intervals in his studies he did not spend in play or idleness, as other children, but would be always inventing or arranging some **oration or declamation** to himself, the subject of which was generally the excusing or accusing his companions, so that his **master** would often say to him, "You, my boy, will be nothing small, but great one way or other, for good or else for bad." He received reluctantly and carelessly instructions given him to improve his manners and behaviour, or to teach him any pleasing or graceful accomplishment; but whatever was said to improve him in **sagacity**, or in management of affairs, he would give attention to, beyond one of his years, from confidence in his natural capacities for such things.

This was the cause, that being mocked afterwards by some that had studied the liberal and elegant amusements, he was driven for revenge and his own defense, to answer with great and stout words, saying that indeed he could offer no skill to tune a harp, nor a viol, nor to play of a **psaltery**: but if they did put a city into his hands that was of small name, weak, and little, he knew ways enough how to make it noble, strong, and great.

Nevertheless, **Stesimbrotus** writeth that **Themistocles** went to Anaxagoras' school of philosophy, and that under **Melissus** he studied **natural philosophy**. But **Melissus was captain of the Samians against Pericles**, at what time he did lay siege unto the city of **Samos**. Now this is true, Pericles was much younger than Themistocles, and Anaxagoras dwelt with Pericles in his own house. They, therefore, might rather be credited who report that Themistocles was an admirer of **Mnesiphilus** the **Phrearrhian**, who was neither rhetorician nor natural philosopher, but a professor of that which was then called "wisdom"; which was no other thing but **a certain knowledge to handle great causes**, and an endeavour to have a good wit and judgment in matters of state and government.

Part Two

In the first part of his youth he was not regular nor happily balanced; he allowed himself to follow mere natural character, which, without the control of reason and instruction, is apt to hurry, upon either side, into sudden and violent courses, and very often to break away and determine upon the worst; as he did afterwards confess himself by saying that a ragged colt ofttimes proves a good horse, specially if he be well ridden, and broken as he should be.

Howsoever it was, it is most true that Themistocles earnestly **gave himself to state**, and was suddenly taken with desire of glory. For **even at his first entry**, because he would set foot before the proudest, he stood **at pike against** the greatest and mightiest persons that **bore the sway and government**, but more especially against **Aristides**, the son of Lysimachus. They always took contrary part one against another, not only in their private likings, but also in the government of the commonwealth.

[omission for mature content]

For Aristides, being by nature a very good man, a just dealer, and honest of life, and one that in all his doings would never flatter the people, nor serve his own glory, but rather to the contrary would do, would say, and would counsel always for the most benefit and commodity of the commonwealth, was ofttimes enforced to resist Themistocles, and disappoint his ambition, Themistocles being ever busily moving the people to take some new matter in hand. For it is said that Themistocles was so transported with the thoughts of glory, and so inflamed with the passion for great actions, that, though he was still young during the **Battle of Marathon**, where there was no talk but of the worthiness of **Captain Miltiades** that had won the battle: he was found many times solitarily there alone, thoughtful and reserved; besides, they say he could then take no rest in the night, neither would go to plays in the daytime, nor would keep company with those whom he was accustomed to be familiar withal before. Furthermore, he would tell them that wondered at the change, and asked him what he ailed, that Miltiades' victory would not let him sleep. And when others were of opinion that the Battle of Marathon would be an end to the war, Themistocles thought that it was but the beginning of far great conflicts, and for these, to the benefit of all Greece, he kept himself in continual readiness, and his city also in proper training, foreseeing from far before what would happen.

Narration and Discussion

The lifelong differences between Aristides and Themistocles are already apparent. As a **creative narration**, draw, write, or act out their contrasting characters.

Creative narration #2: Write a school report card for Themistocles (or imagine a parent-teacher interview).

For older students: Plutarch says that Themistocles deliberately challenged barriers between the "ins" and the "outs," for instance by persuading boys from the "in" class to exercise with him. How might Themistocles' experiences as an outsider have inspired or shaped his career in politics?

For further thought: Plutarch says that "natural character...without the control of reason and instruction, is apt to hurry, upon either side, into sudden and violent courses, and very often to break away and determine upon the worst." Why is education important in "taming" our natural character? What other forces may also influence it? (See 1 Corinthians 2:14 and 15:46; Ephesians 4:22-24.)

Lesson Two

Introduction

The Persians had been quiet after Marathon, but might return at any time. Themistocles, who had dreamed of being a respected leader, suddenly had almost more responsibility than he could handle. When a new source of income appeared, he knew what to do with it: but could he convince the Athenians that his idea would work?

Vocabulary

revenue: income, profits

a hundred galleys: Themistocles wanted two hundred, but he was forced to compromise

overcome him by sea: at the **Battle of Salamis** (Plutarch is getting ahead of the story a bit)

bend their force to sea: build up their naval power

cast it in his teeth: reproach him

the bench and the oar: The galleys were powered by banks (or benches) full of men with oars. The critics said that he had changed the Athenians from proud soldiers into galley slaves.

when he saw his army by sea broken…: that is, after the **Battle of Salamis**

he fled straight upon it: he ran away as fast as possible

liberal: generous

plentiful revenue: large income

miserable: miserly

passion for distinction: desire for recognition and glory

lute: a stringed musical instrument

frequent his company: want to be with him

equipage: his chariot, horses, and attendants

keep the strait: guard against invasion through that route

People

Darius: Darius I ("the Great") ruled Persia until 486 B.C. He was succeeded by his son **Xerxes I**.

Eurybiades: a Spartan naval commander

Historic Occasions

486 B.C.: Xerxes became king of Persia

483 B.C.: Themistocles persuaded the Athenians to build ships

482 B.C.: Aristides ostracized

481 B.C.: Thirty Greek city-states formed alliance against the Persians

480 B.C.: Battle of Artemisium (described in more detail later)

On the Map

Aegina, the **Aeginetes:** Aegina is an island near Athens.

Thessaly: a region of northern Greece

Artemisium: a cape or headland in northern **Euboea**

Reading

Part One

Wherefore, where the citizens of Athens before did use to divide among themselves the **revenue** of their mines of silver, which were in a part of Attica called Laurium: he alone was the first that dared speak to the people, to persuade them that from thenceforth they should cease that distribution among themselves, and employ the money of the same in making of galleys, to make wars against the **Aeginetes**. For their wars against all Greece were most cruel, because they were lords of the sea, and had so great a number of ships. This persuasion drew the citizens more easily to Themistocles' mind, than threatening them with **King Darius** or the Persians would have done: who were far from them, and not feared that they would come near unto them.

So this opportunity taken of the hatred and jealousy between the Athenians and the Aeginetes made the people to agree that with the said money they would make **a hundred galleys**, with which they fought against **King Xerxes**, and did **overcome him by sea**.

Part Two

Now after this good beginning and success, Themistocles won the citizens by degrees to **bend their force to sea**, declaring unto them how by land they were scant able to make head against their equals, whereas by their power at sea they should not only defend themselves from the barbarous people, but moreover be able to command all Greece. Hereupon he made them "good mariners and passing seamen," as Plato sayeth, where before they were stout and valiant soldiers by land.

This gave his enemies occasion to **cast it in his teeth** afterwards that he had taken away the Athenians' spear and shield, and had brought them to **the bench and the oar.** Now whether thereby he did overthrow the justice of the commonwealth or not, I leave that to the philosophers to dispute. But that the preservation of all Greece stood at that time upon the sea, and that the galleys only were the cause of setting up Athens again: **Xerxes** himself is a sufficient witness, besides other proofs that might be brought thereof. For his army by land being yet whole, and unset on, **when he saw his army by sea broken, dispersed, and sunk, he fled straight upon it**, confessing, as it were, that he was now too weak to deal any more with the Grecians.

Themistocles is said to have been eager in the acquisition of riches, according to some, so that he might be the more **liberal**; for loving to sacrifice often, and to be splendid in his entertainment of strangers, he required a **plentiful revenue**. Others, to the contrary, blame him much, that he was too **miserable**: for some say, he would sell presents of meat that were given him.

He went beyond all men in the **passion for distinction**. When he was still young and unknown in the world, he entreated Episcles of Hermione, who had a good hand at the **lute** and was much sought after by the Athenians, to come and practise at home with him, being ambitious of having people inquire after his house and **frequent his company**. When he came to the Olympic games, and was so splendid in his **equipage** and entertainments, in his rich tents and furniture, he displeased the Greeks, who thought that such magnificence might be allowed in one who was a young man and of a great family, but was a great piece of insolence in one as yet undistinguished, and without title or means for making any such display.

Part Three

[Omission for length: Themistocles became so powerful that, first, he managed to have Aristides ostracized; and he then was elected general of the Athenians. They first persuaded Themistocles to lead a land army to defend the region of ***Thessaly****; but when that was not very successful, they agreed to put his naval plan to a test.]*

Whereupon they sent him with their navy to the city of **Artemisium**, to **keep the strait**. There the other Grecians would have had the Lacedaemonians and their admiral **Eurybiades** to have had the authority and commandment of the rest. But the Athenians would not set sail under any other admiral than their own, because theirs were the greatest number of ships in the army, and above all the other Grecians. Themistocles foreseeing the danger that was likely to fall out amongst themselves, did willingly yield the whole authority unto Eurybiades, and got the Athenians to agree unto it: assuring them that if they behaved themselves valiantly in these wars, the other Grecians of their own accord would afterwards submit themselves unto their obedience. Hereby it appeareth that he only of all others was at that time the original cause of the saving of Greece, and did most advance the honour and glory of the Athenians, by making them to overcome their enemies by force, and their friends and allies with liberality.

Narration and Discussion

How did Themistocles handle the Athenians' reluctance to serve under another general? Does this seem surprising, given Themistocles' love of "distinction?"

For older students: "Hereby it appeareth that he only of all others was at that time the original cause of the saving of Greece, and did most advance the honour and glory of the Athenians, by making them to overcome their enemies by force, and their friends and allies with liberality." Discuss this saying, and particularly the ending: were the Athenians' "friends and allies" winners, or losers?

For further thought: Plutarch says that Themistocles made the Athenians "good mariners and passing seamen," since they could no longer dominate in land warfare. Did he take away something as well, as the critics said?

Lesson Three

Introduction

The opportunity to show off Greek naval power at the Battle of Artemisium was interrupted by news that the Persians had fought their way through the passage at Thermopylae and were marching towards Athens. Themistocles quickly finished emptying the city, using the "walls of wood" prophecy (and some disappearing snakes) to hurry people onto the transport ships.

Vocabulary

armada: fleet of ships

good sum of money: Themistocles collected enough money to bribe Eurybiades to stay and fight.

the fight at Artemisium; when they went by sea to Artemisium: In an attempt to block the Persians from entering southern Greece, Themistocles sent the entire Athenian fleet to Artemisium; and this required Athens to be evacuated since it would be left unguarded. The **Battle of Artemisium** lasted three days, and the Greek navy at least held its own. However, the defeat at **Thermopylae** changed the situation, and the Greeks retreated towards **Salamis**.

draw to the Strait of Peloponnesus: the Greek allies intended to concentrate their forces at the Isthmus of Corinth, abandoning Athens to the Persians

leave their city: Those Athenians unable to fight were said to have been evacuated to **Troezen** before the **Battle of Artemisium**, but this seems to have been a final evacuation to the **Island of Salamis**. Historical accounts do not all agree on how many people were moved, or when and where.

frame a device: form a plan or scheme

Athena's snake: Snakes were associated with the goddess Athena and were frequently included in her statues, including that by Phidias in the Parthenon. The snakes referred to here, however, lived in a snake pit and were given "cakes" by temple servants. At this time, the snakes either refused to eat the cakes or had disappeared altogether, which was taken as a sign of Athena's displeasure.

pointing them the way unto the sea: encouraging them to load their ships and evacuate the city

walls of wood: This ambiguous image was interpreted at first to mean building something like a fort, but Themistocles insisted that it referred to ships.

bondmen: servants, slaves

People

King Leonidas: King of Sparta who led the defense of Thermopylae

Artemis: In Greek mythology, the goddess of the hunt, among other things; the Greek equivalent of **Diana**

Historic Occasions

August 480 B.C.: Battle of Artemisium (see note above)

August 480 B.C.: Battle of **Thermopylae**

On the Map

Aphetes or **Aphetae:** a port in Thessaly

Isle of Sciathe or **Sciathus:** an island in the northwest Aegean Sea

Isle of Euboea, Euboeans: Euboea is the second-largest Greek island after Crete.

Thermopylae: a narrow coastal passage, named for nearby hot springs, and famous as the place where Spartan troops held the Persians off for three days before being massacred

Ionia, Ionians: a region of present-day Turkey which had been colonized by the Greeks

Doris, Dorians: a district of Greece bordering on **Phocis**

Phocis, Phocians: a region of central Greece which included Delphi

Boeotia: the region northwest of Attica

Strait of Peloponnesus: the channel between the Peloponnesus and Crete. See note in **Vocabulary**.

Salamis: an island in the Saronic gulf, near Athens

Reading

Part One

As soon as the Persian **armada** arrived at **Aphetae**, Eurybiades was astonished to see such a vast number of vessels before him; and being informed that two hundred more were sailing around behind the **island of Sciathus**, he immediately determined to retire farther into Greece, and to sail back into some part of Peloponnesus, where their land army and their fleet might join; for he looked upon the Persian forces to be altogether unassailable by sea. But the **Euboeans**, fearing that the Greeks would forsake them and leave them to the mercy of the enemy, sent an envoy named Pelagon to confer privately with Themistocles, taking with him a **good sum of money**, which, as

Herodotus reports, he accepted and gave to Eurybiades.

[omission for length]

Part Two

These first fights in the strait of Euboea, between the Grecians and the barbarous people, were not so important as to make any final decision of the war; but it was a taste given unto them which served the Grecians' turn very much, by making them to see by experience, and the manner of the fight, that it was not the great multitude of ships, nor the pomp and the sumptuous setting out of the same, nor the proud barbarous shouts and songs of victory that could stand them to purpose, against noble hearts and valiant-minded soldiers that dared grapple with them, and come hand to hand with their enemies.

This Pindar appears to have seen, and says, justly enough, of **the fight at Artemisium**, that:

> There the sons of Athens set
>
> The stone that freedom stands on yet.

For the first step towards victory undoubtedly is to gain courage.

Sidebar

Artemisium is in Euboea, beyond the city of Histiaea, a sea-beach open to the north; most nearly opposite to it stands Olizon ; there is a small temple there, dedicated to "**Diana** of the Dawn"; and trees about it, around which again stand pillars of white marble; and if you rub them with your hand, they send forth both the smell and colour of saffron. On one of these pillars these verses are engraved:

> With numerous tribes from Asia's region brought
>
> The sons of Athens on these waters fought;
>
> Erecting, after they had quelled the **Mede**,
>
> To **Artemis** this record of the deed.

There is a place still to be seen upon this shore, where, in the middle of a great heap of sand, they take out from the bottom a dark powder like ashes, or something that has passed the fire; and here, it is supposed, the shipwrecks and bodies of the dead were burnt.

Part Three

News being brought what had been done at **Thermopylae**, how that **King Leonidas** was dead, and how that Xerxes had won that entry into Greece by land: they returned back to the interior of Greece, the Athenians having the command of the rear, the place of honour and danger, and much elated by what had been done.

As Themistocles sailed along the coasts, he took notice of the harbours and fit places for the enemy's ships to come to land at, and he engraved large letters in such stones as he found there by change; as also in others which he set up on purpose near to the landing-places, or where they were to water. These were the words:

> "that the **Ionians** should take the Grecians' parts, being their founders and ancestors, and such as fought for their liberty; or at the least they should trouble the army of the barbarous people, and do them all the mischief they could, when the Grecians should come to fight with them."

By these words he hoped either to bring the Ionians to take their part, or at the least he should make the barbarous people jealous and mistrustful of them.

Xerxes being already entered in the uppermost part of the province of **Doris**, into the country of **Phocis**, burning and destroying the towns and cities of the **Phocians**: the other Grecians lay still and suffered the invasion; notwithstanding, the Athenians did request them to meet with the barbarous army in **Boeotia**, to save the country of Attica, as before they had done **when they went by sea to Artemisium**. But they would not hearken to it in no wise, and all was because they were desirous they should **draw to the Strait of Peloponnesus**, and there they should assemble the whole strength and power of Greece within the bar of the same, and make a strong substantial wall from the one sea to the other. The Athenians were enraged to see themselves betrayed, and were half discouraged and out of heart, to see themselves thus forsaken and cast off by the rest of the Grecians. For it was without purpose that they alone should fight against so many thousands of enemies; and therefore their only remedy was to **leave their city**, and cling to their ships; which the people were very unwilling to submit to, imagining that it would signify little now to gain a victory, and not understanding how there could be deliverance any longer after they had once forsaken the temples of their gods, and exposed the tombs and monuments of their ancestors to the fury of their enemies.

Wherefore Themistocles seeing that neither reason nor man's persuasion could bring the people to like his opinion, he began to **frame a device** (as men do use sometimes in tragedies) and to threaten the Athenians with signs from heaven, with oracles and answers from the gods. And the occasion of **Athena's snake** served his tum for a celestial sign and token, which by good fortune did not appear in those days in the temple as it was wont to do: and the priests found the sacrifices, which were daily offered to him, whole and untouched by any. Wherefore being informed by Themistocles what they should do, they spread it abroad amongst the people that the goddess Athena, the protector and defender of the city, had forsaken it, **pointing them the way unto the sea**.

And again he won them by a prophecy, which commanded them to save themselves in **walls of wood**: saying that "walls of wood" did signify nothing else but ships. And for this cause he said, "Apollo, in his oracle, called **Salamis** 'divine,' *not* 'miserable' nor 'unfortunate,' because it should give the name of a most happy victory which the Grecians should get there." And so at the last, they following his counsel, he made this decree: that they should leave the city of Athens to the custody of Athena; and that all those which were of age to carry any weapon should get themselves to the galleys: and for the rest, that every man should see his wife, children, and **bondmen** placed in some sure place as well as he could.

Narration and Discussion

Give a description of Eurybiades. Was his reluctance to fight reasonable?

How did Themistocles persuade the Athenians to leave their city?

Creative narration #1: You are an Ionian, and you come across one of Themistocles' messages in the rocks. Who do you show it to? What do you do?

Creative narration #2: Describe these events from the point of view of the snakes.

Lesson Four

Introduction

Themistocles proved that his skills went beyond military command, by showing true leadership at a time when his city most needed it.

Vocabulary

entertained of the common charge: supported by public funds

obulos, drachmas: units of money

Areopagus: The high council in Athens, like the Roman Senate.

target: shield

feigning: pretending

fardels: bundles (their personal luggage)

would in any case depart from thence: see **Lesson Three**

list: desire

disperse themselves asunder: scatter; divide themselves

betimes: early

therefore that he wished...: Themistocles sent a message encouraging

King Xerxes to attack the non-Athenian mariners as they deserted the Greek coalition and attempted to rejoin their own land army.

On the Map

Troezen: a town in the northeastern Peloponnese

haven of Piraeus: see the **Top Ten Terms** list

Reading

Part One

After this decree was passed and authorized by the people, the most part of them did convey their aged fathers and mothers, their wives and little children, into the city of **Troezen**, where the Troezenians received them very lovingly and gently. For they gave order that they should be **entertained of the common charge**, allowing them apiece two **obulos** a day, and suffered the young children to gather fruit wheresoever they found it: and furthermore they did hire schoolmasters at the charge of the commonwealth, to bring them up at school. He that was the penner of this decree was one called Nicagoras.

The Athenians at that time had no common money; but the **Areopagus** (as Aristotle sayeth) furnished every soldier with eight **drachmas**, which was the only means by which the galleys were armed. Yet Clidemus writeth, that this was a craft devised of Themistocles. The Athenians being come down unto the haven of Piraeus, he made as though the **target** of Pallas (on the which Medusa's head was graven) had been lost, and was not found with the image of the goddess: and **feigning** to seek for it, he ransacked every corner of the galleys, and found a great deal of silver which private persons had hidden amongst their **fardels**. This money was brought out unto the people, and by this means the soldiers that were shipped had the wherewithal to provide them of necessary things.

When the whole city of Athens were going on board, it afforded a spectacle worthy alike of pity and admiration, to see them thus send away their fathers and children before them, and, unmoved with their cries and tears, passed over into the island. But that which stirred compassion most of all was, that many of old men, by reason of their great age, were left behind; and even the tame domestic animals could not be seen without some pity, running about the town and howling, as desirous to be carried along with their masters that had kept them; among which it is reported that Xanthippus, the father of Pericles, had a dog that would endure to stay behind but leaped into the sea, and swam along by the galley's side till he came to the island of Salamis, where he fainted away and died; and that spot in the island which is still called "The Dog's Grave" is said to be his.

Part Two

Among the great actions of Themistocles at this crisis, the recall of Aristides was not the least: for, before the war, he had been ostracized by the party which Themistocles headed, and was in banishment; but now, perceiving that the people regretted his absence, and were fearful that he might go over to the Persians to revenge himself, and thereby ruin the affairs of Greece, Themistocles proposed a decree that those who were banished for a time might return again, to give assistance by word and deed to the cause of Greece with the rest of their fellow-citizens.

And also where Eurybiades, being general of the Grecians' whole army by sea (for the worthiness of the city of Sparta, but otherwise a rank coward at time of need), **would in any case depart from thence**, and retire into the gulf of Peloponnesus, where all the army of the Peloponnesians was by land assembled: in that, Themistocles stood against him, and did hinder it all he could.

Part Three

At that time also it was that Themistocles made so notable answers, which specially are noted and gathered together. For example, Eurybiades said one day unto him: "Themistocles, those that at plays and games do rise before the company are whistled at." "It is true," said Themistocles: "but those that tarry last so do never win any game."

Another time Eurybiades, having a staff in his hand lifted it up as though he would have struck him. "Strike and thou wilt," said he, "so thou wilt hear me." Eurybiades wondering to see him so patient, suffered him then to say what he would. Then Themistocles began to bring him to reason.

And when one who stood by him said unto him: "Themistocles, for a man that hath neither city nor house, it is an ill part to will others that have such things to forsake all." Themistocles turning to him, replied,

> "We have willingly forsaken our houses and walls (said he), cowardly beast that thou art, because we would not become slaves for fear to lose things that have neither soul nor life. And yet our city, I tell thee, is the greatest of all Greece: for it is a fleet of two hundred galleys ready to fight, which are come hither to save you if you **list**. But if you will needs go your ways, and forsake us the second time, you shall hear tell, ere it be long, that the Athenians have another free city, and have possessed again as much good land as that which they have already lost."

[omission for length]

Part Four

But when the fleet of their enemy's ships arrived at the haven of Phaleron, upon the coast of Attica, and with the number of their ships concealed all the shore; and when they saw the king himself in person come down with his land army to the seaside, with all his forces united, then the good counsel of Themistocles was soon forgotten, and the Peloponnesians cast their eyes again towards the isthmus, and took it very ill if any one spoke against their returning home. To be short, it was concluded that they should sail away the next night following, and the masters of the ships had order given them to make all things ready for them to depart.

Themistocles, perceiving their determination, was marvellous angry in his mind that the Grecians would thus **disperse themselves asunder**, repairing every man to his own city, and leaving the advantage which the nature of the place, and the strait of the arm of the sea where they lay in harbour together, did offer them: and so he bethought himself how this was to be helped. Suddenly the practice of one Sicinnus came into his mind, who, being a Persian born, and taken prisoner before in the wars, loved Themistocles very well, and was schoolmaster to his children. This Sicinnus he secretly sent unto the king of Persia, to advertise him that Themistocles (general of the Athenians) was very desirous to become his majesty's servant, and that he did let him understand **betimes** that the Grecians were determined to flee: and **therefore that he wished him not to let them escape, but to set upon them, whilst they were troubled and afraid, and far from their army by land, to the end that upon a sudden he might overthrow their whole power by sea**.

Xerxes, supposing this intelligence came from a man that wished him well, received the messenger with great joy, and thereupon gave present order to his captains by sea that they should instantly set out with two hundred galleys to encompass all the islands, and enclose all the straits and passages, that none of the Greeks might escape, and that they should afterwards follow with the rest of their fleet at leisure.

This being done, Aristides (Lysimachus' son) being the first that perceived it, went to Themistocles' tent, though he was his enemy, and through his only means had been banished before, as ye have heard: and calling him out, told him how they were environed. Themistocles, who knew well enough the goodness of this man, being very glad he came at that time to seek him out, declared unto him the policy he had used by the message of Sicinus, and entreated him that, as he would be more readily believed among the Greeks, he would make use of his credit to help to induce them to stay and fight their enemies in the narrow seas.

Aristides, commending his great wisdom, went to deal with the captains of the other galleys, and to procure them to fight. For all this, they would not credit what he said, until such time as there arrived a galley which brought certain news that the strait, out of doubt, was shut up. So that besides the necessity which did urge them, the spite which the Grecians conceived thereof did provoke them to hazard the battle.

Narration and Discussion

Explain one of Themistocles' "notable answers." How might the person spoken to have reacted?

How did Aristides show both wisdom and courage at this time?

How did the fact that the Grecian mariners tried to get *out* of fighting actually set the stage for the Battle of Salamis?

Lesson Five

Introduction

This lesson describes the **Battle of Salamis**, and then introduces a post-battle problem for Themistocles: would it be wiser to keep the king of Persia within Greek territory and continue to fight things out, or to let him go on his way? And how might he be convinced to leave?

Vocabulary

trow: think, believe

forbearing to: restraining himself from

cumbrous: cumbersome, hard to manage

broadside: "sideways first"

transfixing each the other with their brazen prows: catching the ships onto each other by the projections on their fronts

that glorious and famous victory: the Battle of Salamis

remissness: neglect

expedition: speed and ease

People

Aeschylus the poet: Greek playwright known for his tragedies

Ariamenes: a son of Darius I, also called Ariabignes

Artemisia: Artemisia I of Caria, the queen of Halicarnassus, who fought as an ally of Xerxes, personally commanding her own ships

On the Map

Hellespont: the **strait** between the Aegean and the Sea of Marmara; it was also the only route back to Persia.

Reading

Part One

The next morning by break of day, King Xerxes placed himself on a marvellous steep high hill, from whence he might discern his whole fleet, and the ordering of his army by sea, above the Temple of Hercules, as Phanodemus writeth. This is the place where the coast of Attica is separated from the island by a narrow channel; but Acestodorus writes that it was in the confines of Megara, upon those hills which are called the Horns, where he sat in a chair of gold, with many secretaries about him to write down all that was done in the fight.

[omission for content]

As for the number of the ships of the barbarous navy: **Aeschylus the poet**, in a tragedy which he entitled *The Persians*, knowing certainly the truth, sayeth thus:

> King Xerxes had a thousand ships I know,
> amongst the which, two hundred were (I **trow**)
> and seven: which all the rest did oversail
> with swifter course. This is without fail.

The Athenians had nine score, in every one of the which there were eighteen soldiers, whereof four of them were archers, and all the rest armed men. Themistocles also did with no less skill and wisdom choose his time and place to fight, **forbearing to** charge his enemies, until the hour was come that of ordinary custom the sea wind arose, and brought in a rough tide within the channel, which did not hurt the Grecian galleys, being made low and snug, but greatly offended the Persian galleys, which had high sterns and lofty decks, and were heavy and **cumbrous** in their movements, as it presented them **broadside** to the quick charges of the Greeks, who fiercely set upon them, having always an eye to Themistocles' direction, that best foresaw their advantage.

Ariamenes, admiral to Xerxes, a brave man and by far the best and worthiest of the king's brothers, was seen throwing darts and shooting arrows from his huge galley, as from the walls of a castle. Aminias the Decelean and Sosicles the Pedian, who sailed in the same vessel, upon the ships meeting stem to stern, and **transfixing each the other with their brazen prows**, so that they were fastened together, when Ariamenes attempted to board theirs, ran at him with their pikes, and thrust him into the sea. His body, as it floated amongst other shipwrecks, was known to **Artemisia**, and carried to Xerxes.

[omission for length]

Part Two

The first man of the Athenians that took any of the enemy's ships was Lycomedes, a captain of a galley, who cut down the ship's ensign and dedicated it to Apollo the Laurel-Crowned. The other Grecians in the front being equal in number with the barbarous ships, by reason of the straitness of the arm of the sea wherein they fought, and so straitened as they could not fight but by one and one, where by the barbarians disorderly laid one another aboard, that they did hinder themselves with their over-multitude: and in the end were so sore pressed upon by the Grecians, that they were constrained to flee by night, after they had fought and maintained battle until it was very dark.

So the Grecians won **that glorious and famous victory**: of the which may truly be affirmed that, as Simonides sayeth:

Was never yet, nor Greek nor Barbarous crew

that could by sea, so many men subdue:
Nor that obtained, so famous victory
in any fight, against their enemy.

Thus was the victory won through the valiantness and courage of those that fought that battle, but especially through Themistocles' great policy and wisdom.

Part Three

After this battle, Xerxes, being mad for his loss, thought to fill up the arm of the sea, and to pass his army by land, upon a bridge, into the Isle of Salamis. Themistocles, because he would feel Aristides' opinion, told him, as they were talking together, that he thought best to go and occupy the **strait of Hellespont** with the navy, to break the bridge of ships which Xerxes had caused to be made: "to the end," said he, "that we may take Asia into Europe." Aristides liked not this opinion.

> "We have hitherto fought with an enemy who has regarded little else but his pleasure and luxury; but if we shut him up within Greece, and drive him to necessity, he that is master of such great forces will no longer sit quietly with an umbrella of gold over his head, looking upon the fight for his pleasure; but in such a strait will attempt all things; he will be resolute, and appear himself in person upon all occasions, he will soon correct his errors, and supply what he has formerly omitted through **remissness**, and will be better advised in all things. There, it is no ways our interest, Themistocles, to take away the bridge that is already made, but rather to build another, if it were possible that he might make his retreat with the more **expedition**."

Themistocles then replied, "Seeing you think this were good to be done, we must all lay our heads together, to rid ourselves of him as soon as may be."

Narration and Discussion

Imagine that years have gone by in Athens, and you are telling your grandchildren about the Battle of Salamis. What questions might they ask, and how would you answer?

Creative narration for older students: Shakespeare borrowed stories and sometimes whole lines from Plutarch. How might he have written the discussion between Themistocles and Aristides?

Lesson Six

Introduction

Having seen the last of the Persians, the Greeks took the opportunity to celebrate. ("Who gets the bravery medal?" "I do!" said everyone.)

Vocabulary

confederates: the allies of Athens

voices: votes

anecdotes: stories

cast him in the teeth: mocked him

indulge: spoil, give in to his demands

conceits: his sayings and metaphors

Historic Occasions

Winter 480-479 B.C.: The Athenians were able to return to their city, which had been badly damaged by the Persians

479 B.C.: Battle of Plataea

On the Map

Seriphos: or Serifos; an island in the Aegean Sea

Reading

Part One

Themistocles found out among the captives one of the King of Persia's (personal servants), named Arnaces, whom he sent to the king, to inform him that the Greeks, being now victorious by sea, had decreed to sail to the Hellespont, where the boats were fastened together, and destroy the bridge; but that Themistocles, being concerned for the king, revealed this to him, that he might hasten towards the Asiatic seas, and pass over into his own dominions; and in the meantime would cause delays and hinder the **confederates** from pursuing him. Xerxes no sooner heard this but, being very much terrified, he proceeded to retreat out of Greece with all speed.

The prudence of Themistocles and Aristides in this was afterwards more fully understood at the **Battle of Plataea**, where the Persian lieutenant Mardonius, with a very small fraction of the forces of Xerxes, put the Greeks in danger of losing all. Of all the towns and cities that fought there, Herodotus writeth that the city of Aegina won the fame for valiantness above the rest; and of private men, among the Grecians, Themistocles was judged the worthiest man: although it was sore against their wills, because they envied much his glory. When they returned to the entrance of Peloponnesus, where the several commanders having sworn upon the altar of their sacrifices that they would give their **voices**, after their consciences, to those they thought had best deserved it: everyone gave himself the first place for worthiness, and the second unto Themistocles. The Lacedaemonians carried him into Sparta, where, giving the rewards of valour to Eurybiades, and of wisdom and conduct to Themistocles, they crowned him with olive, presented him with the best chariot in the city, and moreover they sent three hundred young men to accompany him to the confines of their country. And at the next Olympic games, when Themistocles was once come into the showplace where these games were played, the people looked no more on them that fought, but all cast their eyes on him, shewing him to the strangers which knew him not, with their fingers, and by clapping of their hands did witness how much they esteemed him. Whereat he himself took so great delight, that he confessed to his friends that he then reaped the fruit of all his labours for the Greeks.

Part Two

He was, indeed, by nature, a great lover of honour, as is evident from the **anecdotes** recorded of him. When chosen admiral by the Athenians, he would not quite conclude any single matter of business, either public or private, but deferred all till the day they were to set sail, that, by dispatching a great quantity of business all at once, and having to meet a great variety of people, he might make an appearance of greatness and power.

[omission for length]

He said the Athenians did not esteem of him in time of peace: but when any storm of wars were toward, and they stood in any danger, they ran to him then, as they run to the shadow of a plane tree upon any sudden rain; and after fair weather come again, they cut away then the branches, and boughs thereof.

There was a man born in **Seriphos**, who being fallen out with him, did **cast him in the teeth**, that it was not for his worthiness, but for the noble city wherein he was born, that he had won such glory. "Thou sayest true," said he; "but neither should I ever have won any great honour, if I had been a Seriphian, nor thou also if thou hadst been an Athenian."

Another time one of the generals having done good service unto the commonwealth, made boast before Themistocles, and compared his service equal with his. Themistocles, to answer him, told him a pretty tale. That the Working Day (*or, the Day After the Festival*) brawled on a time with the Holy Day (*or, the Festival*), repining against her, that he laboured for his living continually, and how she did nothing but fill her belly, and spend that which they had gotten. "Thou hast reason," said the Holy Day. "But if I had not been before thee, thou hadst not been here now. And so, if I had not been then, where had you my masters been now?"

Laughing at his own son, who got his mother, and, by his mother's means, his father also, to **indulge** him, he told him that he had the most power of anyone in Greece: "For," sayeth he, "the Athenians command the Grecians, I command the Athenians, my wife commandeth me, and my son commandeth her."

[omission for length]

These were Themistocles' pleasant **conceits** and answers.

Narration and Discussion

What happened after the battle? How did the Greeks make Xerxes *want* to get out of their country quickly?

Themistocles was accused that it was "not for his worthiness, but for the noble city wherein he was born, that he had won such glory." Do you agree? What was his response?

Creative narration: Choose one of Themistocles' stories or sayings, and illustrate it or act it out.

Lesson Seven

Introduction

The Athenians were just repairing the damages, they claimed…or were they taking the opportunity to build more power than they had ever had? Nobody seemed quite sure.

Vocabulary

ephors: Spartan officials

charging him with rebuilding the walls: The official Spartan objection to rebuilding the walls of Athens, or any northern city, was that the Persians might come back and use it as a fortress.

the fable of the goddess Pallas: "The Contest of Poseidon and Athena," in Greek mythology. The two deities both wanted to be patron of Athens. Poseidon/Neptune, the god of the sea, offered water, but as it was salty it seemed useless for the people. The winner was Athena's gift of the olive tree.

prevailed, and obtained the preeminence: won the contest and became patron of Athens

Thirty Tyrants: the pro-Spartan government established at the end of the war, in 404 B.C.

hustings: speeches, orations

oligarchy: government by a small group

arsenal: place where weapons and other military equipment are kept

People

Aristophanes: a playwright in ancient Athens

On the Map

Pagasae: a town in Magnesia, in the region of Thessaly

Reading

Part One

After these things, Themistocles began to rebuild and fortify the city of Athens; bribing, as Theopompus reports, the Lacedaemonian **ephors** not to be against it, but, as most relate it, overreaching and deceiving them. For, under the pretext of an embassy, he went to Sparta; whereupon, the Lacedaemonians **charging him with rebuilding the walls,** he denied the fact, bidding them to send people to Athens to see whether it were so or no; by which delay he got time for the building of the wall, and also placed these ambassadors in the hands of his countrymen as hostages for him; and so, when the Lacedaemonians knew the truth, they did him no hurt, but, suppressing all display of their anger for the present, sent him away.

Afterwards he made them also mend and fortify the haven of Piraeus, having considered the situation of the place, and all to incline the city to the sea. Wherein he did directly contrary to all the counsel of the ancient kings of Athens: who, seeking (as they say) to withdraw their people from the sea, and to accustom them to live upon the land, by planting, sowing, and plowing their grounds, did tell them **the fable of the goddess Pallas**. And that is this, how she, contending with Neptune about the patronage of the country of Athens, brought forth and shewed to the judges the olive tree, by means whereof she **prevailed, and obtained the preeminence.**

Even so, Themistocles did not join the haven of Piraeus unto the city of Athens (as the comical poet **Aristophanes** sayeth), but rather joined the city unto the haven, and the land unto the sea. This increased the power and confidence of the people against the nobility; the authority coming into the hands of sailors and boatswains and pilots. Thus it was one of the orders of the **Thirty Tyrants** (*a few years later*) that the **hustings** in the assembly should be turned round towards the land; implying their opinion that the empire by sea had been the origin of the democracy, and that the farming population were not so much opposed to **oligarchy**.

Part Two

Themistocles called to mind another matter also of greater importance, to make the city of Athens a greater power by sea. For after the retreat of Xerxes, when all the fleet and navy of the Grecians wintered in the haven of **Pagasae**: he said one day in an open assembly of the people, that he had thought of a thing which would be very profitable and beneficial for them, but it was not to be told openly. The people willed him then to impart it to Aristides: and if he thought it good, they would execute it speedily.

Themistocles then told Aristides that the thing he had considered of was to burn the **arsenal** where the Grecians' navy lay, and to set on fire all their ships. Aristides hearing his purpose, returned to the people, and told them how nothing could be more profitable, but withal more unjust, than that which Themistocles had devised. The Athenians then willed Aristides it should be let alone altogether.

Narration and Discussion

Describe the things that were happening in Athens at this time. Another historian, Diodorus, wrote that Themistocles created financial incentives to attract merchants and artisans; and that he had even more ships built. Were the Lacedaemonians right to be nervous?

Why did the Athenians ask Themistocles to tell his great idea to Aristides first?

For further thought: Why did the Thirty Tyrants, later on, force those making public speeches to face inland rather than towards the sea? What special point is Plutarch trying to make here?

Lesson Eight

Introduction

The Athenian suspicions of Themistocles' intentions grew worse, and his days in the sunshine came to a sudden end.

Vocabulary

Council of the Amphictyonis: a meeting of Greek states

exacting money of the inhabitants: taxing them

galled him to the quick: made him very angry

verses: rude songs

intimating: insinuating; hinting

aspect: appearance

pluck down: lessen, trim. **Pluck down their stomachs** might be translated as "reduce their arrogance."

mitigate: lessen, cut back, especially to decrease pain or hardship

went to dwell in Argos: This was still in Greek territory.

detection of Pausanias: The Spartan general **Pausanias** was charged with conspiring with the Persians. The Spartans accused Themistocles as well, which is why he left **Argos** for **Molossia**.

sit on (one's) skirts: hamper someone's actions, or punish them

People

Cimon: Athenian statesman, the subject of Plutarch's *Life of Cimon*

Pausanias: Spartan general suspected of conspiring with the Persians

Historic Events

478 B.C.: Plot by Pausanias against Sparta

478 B.C.: Delian League created: Ionia and the Aegean islands allied with Athens

472/471 B.C.: Ostracism of Themistocles

On the Map

Argos: a city in the Peloponnesus

Reading

Part One

The Lacedaemonians proposed, at the **Council of the Amphictyonis,** that the representatives of those cities which were not (officially) in the league, nor had fought against the Persians, should be excluded. Themistocles, fearing that the Thessalians, with those of Thebes, Argos, and others, being thrown out of the council, (and that then) the Lacedaemonians would become wholly masters of the votes and do what they pleased, supported the deputies of their cities, and prevailed with the members then sitting to alter their opinion on this point; showing them that there were but thirty-one cities which had partaken in the war, and that most of these, also, were very small; (and showing) how intolerable would it be, if the rest of Greece should be excluded, and the general council should come to be ruled by two or three great cities. By this, chiefly, he incurred the displeasure of the Lacedaemonians, whose honours and favours were now shown to **Cimon**, with a view to making him the opponent of the state policy of Themistocles.

He was also burdensome to the confederates, for that he went sailing still to and fro amongst the isles, **exacting money of the inhabitants** of the same. And this is to be known by the matter propounded by him to the Andrians (of whom he requested money) and by the answer they made him, as Herodotus writeth. Themistocles said that he had brought them two mighty gods: Love and Force. And they answered him again, that they also had two great goddesses, which kept them from giving him any money: Poverty and Impossibility.

And Timocreon the Rhodian poet **galled him to the quick**, when he sharply taunted him for calling home again (for money) many that were banished; and how for covetousness of money he had betrayed and forsaken his host and friend. The **verses** wherein this matter is mentioned are to this effect:

Who might commend worthy **Pausanias**,

Xanthippus, or good Leotychides,

yet shall I seem but light thereof to pass,

compared with valiant Aristides.

[omission for length]

Besides these verses, Themistocles' own citizens, for the ill-will they bore him, were contented to hear him ill spoken of. Therefore while he sought ways to redress all this, he was driven to use such means, which more increased their hatred toward him. For in his orations to the people, he did oft remind them of the good service he had done them; and perceiving how they were offended withal, he was driven to say, "Why, are ye weary so oft to receive good by one man?"

He yet more provoked the people by building a temple to "Diana of Best Counsel"; **intimating** thereby, that he had given the best counsel, not only to the Athenians, but to all Greece. He built this temple near his own house, in the district called Melite. There is to this day a small figure of Themistocles in the temple of "Diana of Best Counsel," which represents him to be a person not only of a noble mind, but also of a most heroic **aspect**.

Part Two

In the end, the Athenians banished him from Athens for five years, because they would **pluck down** his over great courage and authority; as they did use to serve those whose greatness they thought to be more than the common equality that ought to be among citizens would bear. For this manner of banishment for a time, called *Ostracismon*, was no punishment for any fault committed, but a **mitigation** and taking away of the envy of the people, which delighted to **pluck down their stomachs** that too much seemed to exceed in greatness: and by this means they took away the poison of his malice, by diminishing his glory and honour.

So Themistocles, being banished from Athens, **went to dwell in Argos**. (During this time) the **detection of Pausanias** happened, which gave such advantage to his enemies, that they indicted him of treason. Besides this, the Spartans also did **sit on his skirts**, and charged him sorely.

For Pausanias never before revealed to Themistocles the treason he had purposed, although he was his very familiar friend. But after he saw Themistocles was banished, and did take his exile very impatiently: then Pausanias was bold to open his treason to him, to procure him to take his part, and showed him the letters the king of Persia had written to him, and all to stir him up against the Grecians, as against ungrateful and unnatural people. Howbeit Themistocles shook him off, and told him plainly he would be no partner of his treason; though he never revealed his communications, nor disclosed the conspiracy to any man, hoping either he (Pausanias) would give it up, or that shortly his aspirations to things of great danger, and without purpose or possibility, would be discovered by other means.

[The fallout from Pausanias continues in the next lesson.]

Narration and Discussion

Imagine that you are an Athenian trying to explain to someone else (a friend, your elderly neighbour, someone younger?) why Themistocles is being ostracized.

For older students: In **Lesson Six**, Themistocles is quoted as saying that when "the Athenians… stood in any danger, they ran to him then…and after fair weather come again, they cut away then the branches, and boughs thereof." How were his words prophetic?

Creative narration: If Themistocles were to think back over his early life, what might he say about the plans he had made then? What were his best and worst times? What would he say about the people he knew? You can present this in any format you like.

Lesson Nine

Introduction

Themistocles had been accused of treason, but refused to appear for trial; he also heard that the king of Persia was offering a reward for his capture. He took refuge briefly in Corcyra, then in Epirus, and finally in Aeolia; but finally he came to either a brave or a foolish decision: he would ask for mercy and offer his services at the Persian court. (You may recall that a similar plan did not turn out very well for Pompey.) Getting there, however, would take some strategizing.

Vocabulary

pains of death: see note in previous lesson

at suit and strife: in conflict

suing: formally requesting; appealing (for something)

only for a cloak: as a way of justifying his actions

People

Molossians: one of the major tribes of Epirus, ruled at that time by **King Admetus** and **Queen Phthia**. Famous Molossians include Olympias, mother of Alexander the Great; and Pyrrhus, subject of Plutarch's *Life of Pyrrhus.*

Historic Occasions

470 B.C.: Death of Pausanias

468 B.C.: Death of Aristides

On the Map

Corcyra: or Korkyra, or Corfu; an island in the Ionian Sea

Epirus: a region in the northwest area of ancient Greece

Cyme: a port in Aeolia

Reading

Part One

After Pausanias was condemned, and had suffered **pains of death** for the same: they found, amongst his papers, certain writings and letters, which made Themistocles to be very sore suspected. Whereupon the Lacedaemonians on the one side cried out of him and his enemies and ill-willers at Athens accused him on the other side. To the which he made answer by letters from the beginning, and wrote unto the people that it was not likely that he, who sought all the ways to rule, and was not born to serve, neither had any mind thereto, would ever have thought in his head to sell his own liberty, and the Grecians also, unto the barbarous people their enemies.

Notwithstanding this, the people, being persuaded by his accusers, sent officers to take him and bring him away to be tried before a council of the Greeks, but, having timely notice of it, he passed over into the island of **Corcyra**, because the city there was greatly beholden to him for a certain pleasure in time past he had done them. For they being **at suit and strife** with the Corinthians, he took up the matter between them, and gave judgement on their side, and condemned the Corinthians to pay them twenty talents in damages: and did set down an order that they should occupy the Isle of Leucade in common together, as ground that had been inhabited with the people as well of the one city as of the other.

From thence he fled to **Epirus**, whether being followed by the Athenians, and the Lacedaemonians, he was compelled to venture himself upon a doubtful and very dangerous hope. For he went to yield himself into the hands of **Admetus**, king of the **Molossians**. Who, having heretofore made certain requests unto the Athenians, and being shamefully denied them by means of Themistocles (who then was at his chiefest height and authority), the king was marvellously offended with him: and it was a clear case indeed, that if he could then have laid hands on him, he would have been revenged of him thoroughly.

Howbeit, feeling the present misery of his exile, he thought he might less fear the king's old quarrel and displeasure than the fresh hate and envy of his countrymen. Whereupon he went unto King Admetus, trusting to his mercy, and became an humble suitor to him in a strange, extraordinary way. For he took the king's little young son in his arms, and went and kneeled down before the altar in his chapel: which humble manner of **suing** the Molossians take to be most effectual, and such as they dare not deny, nor refuse. Some say that **Queen Phthia** herself, the king's wife, did inform Themistocles of this their country custom and manner, and brought her little son also near unto the altar. Other write also, that it was Admetus himself that taught and showed him this enforcing manner of petition, **only for a cloak** to excuse himself to those that should come to demand Themistocles of him: he was able to say that by duty of religion he was so straitly bound and restrained, that he might not deliver Themistocles out of his protection.

Part Two

[omission for length: Themistocles continued his travels into Asia]

When Themistocles arrived at **Cyme**, and understood that all along the coast there were many lying in wait for him, for the game was worth the hunting for such as were thankful to make money by any means, the king of Persia having offered by public proclamation two hundred talents to him that should take him; he fled to Aegae, a small city of the Aeolians, where no one knew him but only his host Nicogenes, who was the richest man in Aeolia, and well known to the great men of Inner Asia.

Themistocles continued hidden certain days in his house: in which time, on a night after the feast of a sacrifice, one Olbius, schoolmaster to Nicogenes' children, by some secret working of the gods, suddenly fell into a sort of frenzy, and began to sing these verses out aloud:

> Night shall speak, and night instruct thee,
>
> By the voice of night conduct thee.

The next night following, Themistocles being fast asleep in his bed, dreamed that a snake wound itself round about his belly, and glided upwards to his neck, until it touched his face, and suddenly then it became an eagle, and embraced him with his wings: and so at length did lift him up into the air, and carried him a marvellous way off, until he thought he saw a golden rod (such as heralds used to carry in their hands) whereupon the eagle did set him, and so was delivered of all this fear and trouble he thought himself in.

[Themistocles wanted to appear before the king of Persia, but he didn't want to be caught by bounty hunters on the way. How was he to get there safely?]

Nicogenes had the following device in his head: the barbarous nations for the most part (and specially the Persians) are of a very strange nature, and marvellous jealous over their women, which they keep so straitly locked up, that no man ever seeth them abroad at any time, but are always, like house-doves, kept within doors. And when they have any occasion to go into the country, they are carried in closed coaches covered all about, that no man can look into them. Themistocles was conveyed into one of these coaches, dressed after this manner, and he had warned his men to answer those they met by the way, that asked whom they carried: how it was a young Grecian gentlewoman of the country of Ionia, which they carried to the court to be married to a nobleman there.

Narration and Discussion

How did Themistocles react to being (he insisted) unjustly accused? If you were his lawyer, what case would you give for his innocence?

Creative narration: Retell or dramatize the scene with King Admetus and Queen Phthia in any way you like. You might tell it from the viewpoint of a minor character, as Jill Paton Walsh does in *Children of the Fox* (see introductory notes).

For further thought #1: King Admetus put aside his personal resentment of Themistocles and gave him refuge (and also money for his journey). Why do you think he did so?

For further thought #2: Themistocles' old "frenemy" Aristides died during this time. If he had lived longer, might his influence in Athens have changed events?

Lesson Ten

Introduction

When Themistocles arrived at the Persian court, he used his best skills in rhetoric to approach the king. (Although we don't know how long Themistocles' journey took, historians believe that he was meeting with Artaxerxes I.)

Vocabulary

name: reputation

mean: instrument, method

repair: coming, visit

they did not follow you: The king who was not "followed" was Xerxes, not his successor, but Plutarch admitted that he was not quite sure which king Themistocles was now dealing with.

thralldom: slavery

choler: anger

People

Artabanus: Artabanus was not simply a guard at the door; he had designs on the throne of Persia, was (most likely) the murderer of **Xerxes I**, and was soon put to death himself by **Artaxerxes I**.

Historic Occasions

465 B.C.: Xerxes I assassinated; **Artaxerxes I** became king of Persia. (**Bible Trivia:** Xerxes I, also called Ahasuerus, is believed to have been the king in the Book of Esther. Artaxerxes I is probably the king mentioned in the Books of Ezra and Nehemiah.)

Reading

Part One

Themistocles being come now to the sword's point (as it were) and to the extremity of his danger: he did first present himself unto one **Artabanus**, colonel of a thousand men, and said unto him:

> "Sir, I am a Grecian born, and desire to
> speak with the king: I have matters of
> importance to open to his majesty, and such
> as I know he will thankfully receive."

Artabanus answered him in this manner:

> "My friend sir stranger, the laws and

customs of men are diverse, and some take one thing for honest, others some another thing; but it is most honesty for all men to keep and observe the laws and manners of their own country.

"For you Grecians have the **name** to love liberty, and equality above all things: and for us, amongst all the goodly laws and customs we have, we esteem this above the rest: to reverence and honour our king, as the image of the god of nature, who keepeth all things in their perfect life and state. Wherefore, if thou wilt fashion thyself after our manner to honour the king, thou mayest both see him, and speak with him: but if thou have another mind with thee, then must thou of necessity use some third person for thy **mean**. For this is the manner of our country: the king never giveth audience to any man that hath not first honoured him."

Themistocles hearing what he said, answered him again:

"My lord Artabanus, the great goodwill I bear unto the king, and the desire I have to advance his glory and power, is the only cause of my present **repair** unto his court: therefore I mean not only to obey your laws (since it hath so pleased the gods to raise up the noble empire of Persia unto this greatness), but will cause many other people also to honour the king, more than there do at this present. Therefore let there be no stay, but that myself in person may deliver to

> the king that I have to say unto him."

"Well," said Artabanus, "whom then shall we say thou art ? For by thy speech it seemeth, thou art a man of no mean state and condition."

Themistocles answered him, "As for that, Artabanus, none shall know before the king himself."

Thus doth Phanias report it.

Part Two

Themistocles being brought to the king's presence, after he had presented his humble duty and reverence to him, stood on his feet, and said never a word, until the king commanded the interpreter to ask him what he was; and he answered:

> "May it please your majesty, O noble King: I am Themistocles the Athenian, a banished man out of my country by the Grecians, who humbly repaireth to your highness, knowing I have done great hurt to the Persians, but I persuade myself I have done them far more good than harm. For I it was that kept the Grecians back: **they did not follow you** when the state of Greece was delivered from **thralldom**, and my native country from danger, and that I knew I stood then in good state to pleasure you. Now for me, I find all men's goodwill agreeable to my present misery and calamity: for I come determined, most humbly, to thank your highness for any grace and favour you shall show me; and also to crave humble pardon, if your majesty be yet offended with me. And therefore license me (most noble King) to beseech you, that taking mine enemies the Grecians for

> witnesses of the pleasures I have done the Persian nation, you will of your princely grace use my hard fortune as a good occasion to show your honorable virtue, rather than to satisfy the passion of your heat and **choler**. For in saving my life, your majestic saveth an humble suitor that put himself to your mercy: and in putting me to death, you shall rid away an enemy of the Grecians."

Having spoken thus these words, he said further, that the gods, by various signs and tokens, had procured him to come to submit himself unto him, and told the king what vision he had seen in his dream in Nicogenes' house; and declared also the Oracle of Jupiter Dodonian, who had commanded him that he should go unto "him that was called as a god," and how he thought it was the person of His Majesty, because that god and he in truth were called both great kings.

The king having thus heard him speak, gave him then no present answer again, notwithstanding he marvellously wondered at his great wisdom and boldness. But afterwards, amongst his familiars, the king said he thought himself very happy to meet with the good fortune of Themistocles coming to him; and so besought his great god Arimanius, that he would always send his enemies such minds, as to banish the greatest and wisest men amongst them. It is reported also he did sacrifice unto the gods, to give them thanks therefore, and disposed himself presently to be merry. Insomuch as dreaming in the night, in the midst of his dream he cried out three times together for joy: "I have Themistocles the Athenian."

Narration and Discussion

Why was it probably a good idea for Themistocles to insist on seeing the king in person?

The king of Persia was delighted to "have" Themistocles; Themistocles was, essentially, a prisoner. Would you have made the same choice?

Creative narration: Write a speech in the style of Themistocles to request something that you want.

Lesson Eleven

Introduction

King Artaxerxes offered Themistocles a comfortable life in Persia, and made him governor of Magnesia. However, there was an uncertainty behind this kindness: what might the king eventually ask in return?

Vocabulary

ill countenance: unfriendly looks

groan: North says "sigh"

two hundred talents: the amount of the reward money

removals of the king's favourites: Although the reign of Artaxerxes I is believed to have been mostly peaceful, there were a few insurrections (including one by his brother), as well as an Egyptian uprising (see **Lesson Twelve**). It is not clear which incident is being described here.

magic: that is, the learning of those called the Magi

lay a long time in the city of Magnesia: acting as governor there

People

Demaratus: a Spartan king who had also taken refuge in Persia

On the Map

Magnesia: a district in Ionia; also the city there by the same name

Reading

Part One

The next morning, the king having sent for the chiefest lords of his court, he made Themistocles also to be brought before him: who looked for no goodness at all, specially when he saw the soldiers at the court gates give him **ill countenance** and language both, when they beheld him and understood his name. As he came forward towards the king, who was seated, the rest keeping silence, passing by Roxanes, a commander of a thousand men, he heard him, with a slight **groan**, say, without stirring out of his place, "O thou Greekish serpent, subtle and malicious: the king's good fortune hath brought thee hither."

Nevertheless, when he came to the king, and had once again made him a very humble and low reverence, the king saluted him, and spoke very courteously to him, saying:

> "I am now your debtor of **two hundred talents**, for presenting yourself. It is good reason I should deliver you the money promised him that should have brought you: but I give you a further warrant: be bold, I charge you, and speak your mind freely, say what you think of the state of Greece."

Themistocles replied that a man's discourse was like to a rich Persian carpet, the beautiful figures and patterns of which can only be shown by spreading and extending it out; when it is contracted and folded up, they are obscure and lost; and, therefore, he desired time.

The king liked his comparison passingly well, and willed him to appoint his own time. Themistocles asked a year: in which time having prettily learned the Persian tongue, he afterwards spoke to the king himself without any interpreter. So such as were no courtiers thought he only talked with the king of matters of Greece. But there happening, at the same time, great alterations at court, and **removals of the king's favourites**, he drew upon himself the envy of the great people, who imagined that he had taken the boldness to speak concerning them. Thereupon they greatly envied him, and afterwards murmured much against him.

For indeed the king did honour Themistocles above all other strangers whatsoever they were. On a time the king had him out a-hunting with him, he made him see his mother, with whom he grew familiar: and by the king's own commandment he was to hear the disputations of the wise men of Persia touching secret philosophy, which they call **magic**.

Demaratus the Lacedaemonian being at that time in the court of Persia, the king willing him to ask what gift he would, he besought the king to grant him this favour: to license him to go up and down the city of Sardis, with his royal hat on his head, as the kings of Persia do. Mithropaustes, the king's cousin, taking him by the hand, said unto him: "Demaratus, the king's hat thou demandest, and if it were on thy head, it would cover but little wit. Nay, though Jupiter did give thee his lightning in thy hand, yet that would not make thee Jupiter." But the king gave him so sharp a repulse for his unreasonable request, and was so angry with him for it, that it was thought he would never have forgiven him: howbeit Themistocles was so earnest a suitor for him, that he brought him into favour again.

And the report goeth, that the king's successors which have been since that time, under whom the Persians have had more dealings with the Grecians, than in former days: when they would retain any great state or personage of Greece into their service, they wrote unto him, and promised him they would make him greater about them, than ever was Themistocles about Xerxes. That which is written of him, doth also confirm it. For he being stepped up to great countenance and authority, and followed with great trains of suitors after him by reason of his greatness: seeing himself one day very honourably served at his table, and with all sorts of dainty meats, he turned him to his children, and said unto them: "My sons, we should have been undone, if we had not been undone."

[omission for length]

Part Two

When Themistocles came to Sardis, he visited the temples of the gods, and observing, at his leisure, their buildings, ornaments, and the number of their offerings, he saw in the "Temple of the Mother of the Gods" the statue of a (maiden) in brass, two cubits high, called "The Water-Bringer." Themistocles had caused this to be made and set up when he was surveyor of the waters at Athens, out of the fines of those whom he detected in drawing off and diverting the public water by pipes for their private use; and whether he had some regret to see this image in captivity, or was desirous to let the Athenians see in what great credit and authority he was with the king, he entered into a treaty with the governor to persuade him to send this statue back to Athens. This so enraged the Persian officer that he told him he would write the king word of it. Then Themistocles began to be afraid, and was driven to seek to the governor's wives and other women, whom he got by presents of money to entreat him, and so made fair weather again with the governor. But from thenceforth, he took better guard of himself in all his doings, greatly fearing the envy of the barbarous people.

For he progressed not up and down Asia, as Theopompus writeth, but **lay a long time in the city of Magnesia**, quietly enjoying the king's gracious gifts bestowed on him: where he was honoured and reverenced for one of the greatest persons of Persia, whilst the king was elsewhere occupied in the affairs of the high provinces of Asia, and had no leisure to think upon those of Greece.

Narration and Discussion

Why did Themistocles not answer the king directly when asked his opinion about matters in Greece?

Themistocles said, "My sons, we should have been undone, if we had not been undone." What did he mean?

Creative narration: Write a speech for Themistocles when he discovered the statue that had been stolen from Athens during the war.

For further thought: Does Themistocles' rising position in Persia remind you of a story from the Old Testament? Explain.

Lesson Twelve

Introduction

Themistocles knew that someday he would have to deal with the unfinished business between himself and Athens; and "someday" came when the Athenians crossed the sea to support an Egyptian rebellion. But it wasn't his love of Athens that made him falter in supporting Persia's forces; it was his realization that, particularly with Cimon at the head, they would most likely win*, and that would put him in a very awkward position. On the other hand, if he didn't actively support Persia, he might endanger his good standing with the king, or even his life. What was he to do?

*The Egyptian-Athenian forces did win the battle, although the uprising continued for several years and the Egyptian rebels were eventually defeated.

Vocabulary

levy: gather, as for an army

he determined to make such an end of his life: The historian Thucydides disagrees with this story, saying that Themistocles died of natural causes.

taken his leave…: Dryden, "having shaken hands with them all"

sepulchre: tomb

cosmographer: a scientist interested in the nature of the universe

doubled: gone around

masonry: stonework

People

Plato the comedian: not to be confused with Plato the philosopher

Historic Occasions

460/459 B.C.: death of Themistocles, reportedly by suicide (The exact date is unknown)

On the Map

Cyprus: a large island country in the eastern Mediterranean

Cilicia: a region which is now part of Turkey

Reading

Part One

But when news was brought to Themistocles that Egypt was rebelled, by means of the favour and assistance of the Athenians; and that the Grecians' galleys did scour the seas even unto the Isle of **Cyprus**, and unto the coasts of **Cilicia**, and that Cimon had all the sea in subjection: that made him then to bend all his thoughts how to resist the Grecians, that their greatness might not turn to his hurt.

Then commissions went out to **levy** men, to assemble captains, and to dispatch posts unto Themistocles at Magnesia, with the king's letters straitly charging him to have an eye to the Grecians' doings, to put him in minds of his promise, and to summon him to act against the Greeks.

Yet this did not increase his hatred nor exasperate him against the Athenians, neither was he in any way elevated with the thoughts of the honour and powerful command he was to have in this war; but judging, perhaps, that the object would not be attained (the Greeks having at that time, besides other great commanders, Cimon in particular, who was gaining wonderful military successes); but chiefly being ashamed to sully the glory of his former great actions, and of his many victories and trophies, **he determined to make such an end of his life** as the fame thereof deserved.

For he made a solemn sacrifice unto the gods, and feasted at the same all his friends. And, after he had **taken his leave of them all**, he drank bulls' blood, as most men think; others say he took a poison which dispatcheth a man in four and twenty hours. And so he ended his days in the city of Magnesia, having lived sixty-five years, most of which he had spent in politics and in wars, in government and command.

It is written, that the king of Persia understanding the cause and manner of his death, did more esteem him afterwards than he did before; and that ever after he continued to use his friends and familiars in very good sort.

[omission for length: the later lives of Themistocles' children]

Part Two

The Magnesians possess a splendid **sepulchre** of Themistocles, placed in the middle of their marketplace. But Diodorus the **cosmographer** says, in his work on *Tombs*, but by conjecture rather than of certain knowledge, that near to the haven of Piraeus where the land runs out like an elbow from the promontory of Alcimus, when you have **doubled** the cape and passed inward where the sea is always calm, there is a large piece of **masonry**, and upon this the Tomb of Themistocles, in the shape of an altar. **Plato the comedian** confirms this, he believes, in these verses:

> Thy tomb is fairly placed upon the strand,
>
> Where merchants still shall greet it with the land;
>
> Still in and out 'twill see them come and go,
>
> And watch the galleys as they race below.

The above is Dryden's version. North translates the last two lines quite differently:

> Sometimes also, it may rejoice to see,
>
> the bloody fights, upon the sea that be.

And furthermore, those of Magnesia did institute certain honours unto the family of Themistocles, which continue yet unto this day. And in my time, another Themistocles also of Athens (with whom I was familiarly conversant in the house of Ammonius the philosopher) did enjoy the same honours.

Narration and Discussion

It was illegal to bury an Athenian traitor in Attica, which is one reason for the belief that Themistocles was buried in Magnesia. Should he have been scorned as a traitor, or praised as a hero?

Creative narration: Write Themistocles' monologue as he considered which course of action to take. This could also be written as a conversation between Themistocles and someone else.

Examination Questions

Younger Students:

1. What do you know of Themistocles as a boy?
2. Why did Themistocles desire to speak with the king of Persia? Describe the interview.
3. (alternative) Tell a) how Themistocles saved Athens from the Persians, or b) how he was honoured by the Persians in his banishment.

Older Students:

1. Why and by what steps did Themistocles persuade the Grecians to become "good mariners and passing seamen?" Describe briefly what happened at Salamis.
2. (alternative) Why did Themistocles go to Persia? Give some account of him at the Persian court.
3. **For high school students:** Compare and contrast the character of Themistocles and of Aristides. Give examples to show how Themistocles "earnestly gave himself to state."
4. (alternative) What do you know of the childhood of Themistocles? Give instances to show that in later life the child was "father of the man."

Bibliography

Plutarch's Lives of the Noble Greeks and Romans. Englished by Sir Thomas North. With an introduction by George Wyndham. First Volume. London: Dent, 1894. (Themistocles)

Plutarch's Lives of the Noble Greeks and Romans. Englished by Sir Thomas North. With an introduction by George Wyndham. Fourth Volume. London: Dent, 1894. (Pompeius)

Plutarch's Lives: The Dryden Plutarch. Revised by Arthur Hugh Clough, Volume 1. London: J.M. Dent, 1910. (Themistocles)

Plutarch's Lives: The Dryden Plutarch. Revised by Arthur Hugh Clough, Volume 2. London: J.M. Dent, 1910 (Pompey)

About the Author

Anne E. White (www.annewrites.ca) has shared her knowledge of Charlotte Mason's methods through magazine columns, online writing, and conference workshops. She is an Advisory member of AmblesideOnline and the author of *Minds More Awake: The Vision of Charlotte Mason*, as well as other books in The Plutarch Project series.

Printed in Great Britain
by Amazon

75163050R00108